Christian Counseling

101

Christian Counseling

101

Godly Principles to Help You in Time of Need

[signature] Ph. D.

Terrance Jenkins, D-CPC, Ph. D.

Christian Counseling 101

Copyright © 2024 by Terrance Jenkins, D-CPC, Ph. D.

This publication contains the opinions and ideas of the author who intends to offer information of a general nature. Any reliance on the information herein contained is at the reader's discretion.

ISBN 9781300850717

Dedication

This work is dedicated to all those who may be entering any type of ministry service – both the professional clergy as well as the layperson – because God has called all of His people to become 'Therapons' (helpers) of those who are hurting. I pray that the principles taught herein will be a guide for those who want to help others.

Table of Contents

"And I myself also am persuaded of you, my brethren, that you also are full of goodness, filled with all knowledge, able also to admonish (counsel) one another" (Romans 15:14).

Introduction

It is a challenge to write on a subject of such importance, which reaches across such a wide-ranging audience, especially when so many great writers have written extensively on many of the areas upon which I will embark quite briefly. Realizing that nothing is truly original, I have drawn upon the research of many great writers before me, without which I probably could not have produced this work.

Upon reading this manuscript, the president of Therapon University said, "It appears that you have addressed the issues of counseling from Alpha to Omega. Your writing style is quite professional; you are explaining the concepts clearly and concisely, and you have included quotations from the Bible – Well Done!"

My hope and prayer are that those who read this book will be stirred in their heart to get involved in helping hurting people. As Christians, as God's unique people called to be His children, His bride, and His church, we have a responsibility to our fellow man to help them through challenging times. I do not mean that everyone is to be a professional counselor but that everyone can receive training to be able to help some people, some of the time.

I do not think that believers should be sent to ungodly psychiatrists or psychologists for counseling that could and should be given by others of like precious faith. As you read this work with an open mind and a prayerful heart, you will begin to grasp the fundamentals of how to help hurting people where they are.

A word of caution should be expressed here and you will see this again and again as you proceed through your reading of this book: In helping hurting people, do not become discouraged and give up just because of the apparent lack of being able to help everyone or seeming failure to help someone, as happens from time to time. The important thing to keep in mind is the answer to the question – 'Have I done all that I could have done to help the person in need?' If you can truthfully answer that question in the affirmative, then do not fret about the outcome of your counseling or advice. In other words, rest contented with that fact. Remember that some people do not want help – they simply want a pat on the back to tell them that everything is alright. You do what you can and leave the rest to God.

I have heard pastors say that they are not equipped to manage certain cases that come their way. That is a shame! How can God's people be equipped to help each other when the pastors are not equipped or do not feel they are equipped to help their people? How can the pastor, the shepherd of the flock, equip his people to win lost souls and to help each other over the rough times, if that pastor is not equipped? Something is not right with that picture!

Please do not get me wrong. I emphasize that I am not saying, nor do I believe that everyone should be trained by the pastor to become professional counselors. That is what the Bible Colleges and schools of ministry are for – the training of tomorrow's leaders. My personal belief is that all ministers (especially pastors) should have a certain amount of training in the counseling field. It is not enough to say, 'all you need is Jesus.' He is all one needs for salvation but many do not know how to put their total trust in the One most trustworthy and so they need someone trained in the art of Christian Counseling to help them in the areas of emotional, physical, and sexual hurt (among other areas), and the pastor should be able to give godly counsel before the sad situation gets out of control.

Sadly, most pastors do not get such training in this much-needed field of ministry. Sadder still is the fact that most people entering Christian ministry do not seem to want to study this field and feel that it is not necessary, and the Lord will direct them. How can God direct us when we have not been willing to study the subject? II Timothy 2:15 says, *"Study to show yourself approved unto God, a workman who does not need to be ashamed, rightly dividing the Word of Truth."* Also, most schools of higher learning do not include counseling as a part of the program that must be completed before graduation. They concentrate on the theological, biblical, or divinity aspect of the training and leave the counseling alone. At Montreal School of Ministry, we have stipulated that no one will be permitted to graduate unless he/she has completed a minimum of four core counseling courses.

I offer this little book to you which I have based on Christian principles in the hope that it will encourage you to get involved in this vital area of ministry. I believe that it will help you in your personal life as well as help you help others in their struggles. You will note that I continually emphasize the fact that true Christian Counseling will always point the counselee to the Great Counselor – the Lord Jesus Christ. Anything that does not point the counselee to the Lord is not genuine Christian counseling.

Christian Counseling

Christian counseling is distinct from secular counseling. Christian counseling rises to another dimension. "In contrast to psychologically integrated systems, Biblical counseling seeks to carefully discover those areas in which a Christian may be disobedient to the principles and commands of Scripture and to help him learn how to lovingly submit to God's will," reports the International Association of Biblical Counselors.

My hope in authoring this dissertation is that I may be able to address the subject of counseling in such a way that the reader may glean a greater understanding of the vastness of the subject and its varied components. In other words, I want to make you hungry for an area of ministry that for many years, pastors have left to the professional psychologist or psychiatrist. Pastors have been content to take a back seat because they have embraced the lie that they are not equipped to counsel. That is a lie from the pit and many people; both Christian and non-Christian have gone without godly counsel, as a result. I think maybe sadder still is that pastors have sent their people to ungodly psychologists and psychiatrists for counsel that should be provided through the ministry of the church. It is time for pastors and church leaders to rise to the challenge of this all-important ministry and stand in the gap for God's people. It is not right to send the sheep to ravening wolves to get help.

Having said that, I want to begin by quoting a few verses of Scripture as found in the Book of Proverbs. Please note that we shall refer back to these verses from time to time. They are:

1] Proverbs 11:14, *"Where no counsel is, the people fall: but in the multitude of counselors there is safety."*

2] Proverbs 12:15, *"The way of a fool is right in his own eyes: but he that hearkeneth unto counsel is wise."*

3] Proverbs 13:10, *"Only by pride cometh contention: but with the well advised is wisdom."*

4] Proverbs 15:22, *"Without counsel purposes are disappointed: but in the multitude of counselors, they are established."*

Those verses point out the importance and necessity of seeking wise counsel. Let me be quick to point out that we are speaking strictly of wise, godly counsel, though these words may not preface the word 'counsel' every time it is used. The reason for this type of counsel is that there have been and still are many instances of people receiving counsel that is neither wise nor godly. First, I want us to look at a couple of unwise, ungodly, counseling situations from the Word of God, and see the devastating results of it.

Unwise (ungodly) counsel (Balaam)

The first situation of unwise counsel that I want to share concerns the prophet Balaam. Balaam was summoned by Balak, king of Moab, to come and curse the Israelites for him (Numbers 22-31). Balaam, at first refused to go to Balak, but it is quite clear that in his heart he wanted to go, otherwise he would not have gone to seek the Lord several times as to whether or not he should go. He was making a pretense of his unwillingness to go and curse God's people for he was looking at what he could gain by doing what king Balak wanted him to do. As the story unfolds, God intervenes and changes the curse into a blessing. Please note that Balaam was a mercenary prophet. He was self-willed and interested only in what was in it for him. Yet, he was famous in the land. If he were not famous, the king would not have summoned him for such an important task. Listen to what king Balak says to Balaam, *"Come now therefore, I pray thee, and curse these people; for they are too mighty for me: peradventure I shall prevail, that we may smite them, and that I may drive them out of the land: for I know that he whom thou blesses is blessed, and he whom thou cursest is cursed. And the elders of Moab and the elders of Midian departed with the rewards* (diviner's rewards) *of divination in their hand, and they came unto*

Balaam, and spake unto him the words of Balak," (Numbers 22:6-7; cf. Numbers 22:12-22).

Balaam was eloquent in prophecy, but presumptuous in seeking to alter the Divine plan. In other words, he was double-minded, and here is what the Apostle Paul says of such a person in I Corinthians 10:21, *"You cannot drink the cup of the Lord, and the cup of demons: you cannot be partakers of the Lord's Table and of the table of demons."* And James tells us in Chapter One, verse eight, *"A double-minded man is unstable in all his ways."* The result of Balaam being double-minded was that he went home a failure as far as the curse was concerned. Peter, in describing false teachers, said they *"have forsaken the right way, and are gone astray, following the way of Balaam, the son of Beor, who loved the wage of unrighteousness; but was rebuked for his iniquity: the dumb ass speaking with man's voice forbade the madness of the prophet,"* [II Peter 2:15, 16]. Jude says in verse eleven, *"Woe unto them!"* (Speaking of the characteristics of false teachers), *"for they have gone in the way of Cain, and ran greedily after the error of Balaam for reward* (profit)... "

When Balaam found that he could not curse that which God had blessed he gave Balak counsel that would cause Israel to sin, thereby incurring the wrath or judgment of God. This evil counsel is what Moses referred to when he said, *"Have ye saved all the women alive? Behold, these caused the children of Israel, through the counsel of Balaam, to commit trespass against the Lord in the matter of Peor, and there was a plague among the congregation of the Lord,"* (Numbers 31:15-16). In speaking of the counsel that Balaam gave to Balak, Jesus says through John, the Revelator, *"I have a few things against thee because thou hast there them that hold the doctrine of Balaam, who taught Balak to cast a stumbling block* (put an enticement to sin) *before the children of Israel, to eat things sacrificed to idols, and to commit fornication* (sexual immorality), " Revelation 2:14. Balaam gave counsel that caused a grievous sin in Israel and many of the people died as a result. That is not just bad (ungodly) counsel; that is counsel with devastating results.

Ungodly Counsel (Rehoboam)

The second situation that I want to consider is found in I Kings chapter 12, which tells the story of Rehoboam, who had recently been proclaimed king over Israel. (Solomon, Rehoboam's father, who placed a heavy burden of taxes, and so forth, upon the people, had died). Jeroboam, the son of Nebat, who had fled from Solomon in fear, received news of the death of Solomon and returned from exile, in Egypt, to the land of Israel. Upon his return, he and all the people of Israel came to king Rehoboam asking him to make the taxes and workload a little lighter for the people and they would serve him forever. That sounds like a reasonable request to me but watch what happens as the story unfolds.

King Rehoboam sent the people away, telling them to return in three days and he would give them an answer. The king, during these three days, consulted with the old men who gave him wise counsel. They said, *"... if thou wilt be a servant unto this people this day, and wilt serve them, and answer them, and speak good words unto them, then they will be thy servants forever,"* (v.7). You guessed it! Verse eight says, *"But he forsook the counsel of the old men, which they had given to him, and consulted with the young men who had grown up with him, and which stood before him."*

These young men gave the king unwise, ungodly, counsel to which he adhered, which eventually brought about the downfall of the king, the division of the kingdom, and the judgment of God upon the nation. What a different picture we may have had if Rehoboam had listened to the godly counsel of the old men, who had been through various experiences with Solomon, his father.

There are, however, many examples in the Word of God, of godly men seeking wise counsel and as a result did mighty exploits for the Lord. Some of those men were David, (the sweet Psalmist and king of Israel), who accepted the counsel of Hushai (when his son, Absalom arose against him to claim the kingdom for himself), and the rebuke of Nathan the Prophet when he [David] sinned with Bathsheba. In the case of David's sin, which he tried to hide until Nathan reproved him for it, David repented. His prayer is recorded in Psalm 51, where he cries out in agony of soul, *"Have mercy upon me, O God...blot out my transgressions. Wash me thoroughly from my iniquity and cleanse me from my sin. For I acknowledge my transgressions:..."* What a different picture we would have had if David did not heed the wise counsel that he had received. Later, God said of David, *"He is a man after my own heart"* (1 Samuel 14; cf. Acts 13:22).

Hezekiah sought help from Isaiah, the Prophet when the enemy armies came against Judah and Jerusalem in battle. With advice from Isaiah, he encouraged his people, and God delivered him and the city. However, we read that he later did something very foolish, (he showed all his wealth to ungodly people), and was sternly reprimanded for it by the same prophet.

Solomon, (in his early years), asked for wisdom to rule as king and the Lord gave it to him. He had a tender heart and wanted to do the right thing in his service to God for the people. It was not until the later years of his life that Solomon permitted his foreign wives to lead him astray in the worship of idols rather than he leading them to worship the One True God.

We know that these characters all made stupendous mistakes, but they did not let the mistake stop them from doing the will of God, as they knew it. The difference is that they had a heart for God. When we have a heart for the Lord, we have someone to help us in those times when we make a mess of things. The Bible tells us that, *"The steps of a good man are ordered by the LORD: and he delighteth in his way. 24 Though he fall, he shall not be utterly cast down: for the LORD upholds him with his hand,"* Psalm 37:23, 24.

Godly Counsel

Rev. W. E. Vine says that of the nouns for counsel is the Greek word "boule" which is 'counsel, advice,' while the second Greek word is

---

"sumboulos" which indicates "a councillor with," as in Romans 11:34, *"For who hath known the mind of the Lord? Or, who hath been his counselor?*

One of the verbs used for counsel, in the active voice, is "sumbouleuo," meaning "to advise, to counsel," John 18:14, *"gave counsel;"* and in Revelation 3:18, Jesus says to the church at Laodicea, *"I counsel thee."*

"Every purpose is established by counsel: and with good advice make war," Proverbs 20:18. To say that we are human is to say that we have problems. They take many forms, and we often need someone to talk with about them. We do not necessarily want or need professional or pastoral counsel. Such may not be available, and our problem may not be that serious. We may feel awkward about the whole thing but still need someone to talk with. The truth is, whether we admit it or not, we all need godly counsel. The counselor must remember that what a counselee believes will affect how he deals with various difficulties.

That being said, certain questions arise such as:

A) Why should we seek counsel?

B) To whom should we turn for counsel?

C) What kind of person do we want as a counselor? And so forth.

Let us look at each of those questions and see what the Bible says. Our text said, *"Every purpose is established by counsel..."*

Why should we seek counsel?

Simply put, we should seek godly counsel because it is a Biblical command. Others may know more than we do through their own experience, whether through education or through working with others. A counselor may be able to help us work through our confusion because they are less involved and therefore may see the situation more clearly. In addition, the person to whom we turn may not have the blind spots that we have developed in our lives. I have often asked another counselor, pastor, or deacon, to watch my back, so to speak, because sometimes, when we are in the forest, we cannot always see the trees. Proverbs 12:15 says, *"The way of a fool is right in his own eyes: but he who listens to counsel is wise."* Thus, we must never get to the place in life where we think we know all the answers. If so, we set ourselves up for a fall.

To whom should we go for counsel?

In answering our second question of to whom we should turn for counsel, we first go to 1 Thessalonians 5:12-15. Please note: *"And we beseech* (beg) *you, brethren, to know* (to recognize) *them who labor* (work) *among you, and are over you in the Lord, and admonish* (instruct, exhort, counsel) *you;* 13] *and to esteem them very highly in love for their work's sake. And be at peace among yourselves.* 14] *Now we exhort* (instruct, counsel) *you, brethren, warn them that are unruly* (idle, insubordinate), *encourage the faint-hearted* (feebleminded), *support the weak, be patient toward all men.* 15] *See that none render evil for evil unto any man; but ever follow that which is good, both among yourselves and to all men."*

Therefore, the nature, extent, and seriousness of the problem will determine, to a large extent, to whom we turn for guidance. Someone going through a divorce or separation will of necessity seek either someone who has gone through a similar experience or an outside counselor who has experience in dealing with such a traumatic experience. Likewise, someone who has lost a loved one will seek assurance from a family friend, or a pastor. If possible, it would have to be either someone who has gone through a bereavement or the pastor (counselor) who has had experience helping others in this situation. Again, the available resources where a person lives may be a determining factor for the person seeking help.

Romans 15:14 says, *"And I myself also am persuaded of you, my brethren, that you also are full of goodness, filled with all knowledge, able also to admonish* (counsel) *one another."* In seeking a counselor, we need to ask pertinent questions about him/her such as: 1) Is the person doing the counseling spiritual? In other words, is he following Biblical roles and patterns and does he live a lifestyle consistent with the Word of God? 2) Does the person doing the counseling keep confidentiality? A wise counselor must be able to keep things in confidence. Sad to say, it is just as well to put your life on TV, as it is to confide in some pastors and counselors.

The organization that I worked for as a counselor before being disabled hired another counselor who professed to have a degree in psychology though he had never shown his certificate to prove such. That being said, there would be many times that counselees would come to my office, (we both had to work with the same group of counselees), saying that the other counselor had broken his oath of confidentiality. It seemed that everyone in the building knew what was happening in the life of the particular counselee. And though I could not comment one way or the other, I knew what I was told was the truth because other people who should not have known, also revealed many things to me that the counselor had said to them about particular counselees. 3) Has the counselor being considered shown success in the field where counseling is needed? In other words, do not ask someone bankrupt for financial advice. Do not ask someone who is living in a common-law relationship for advice on marriage problems. 4) How do the children, (if there are any), behave? If there are any behavioral problems with the children, it may be symptomatic of other problems within the family. Finally, 5) Does the counselor have the same problem that you have or perhaps a worse one? There is an old saying that *"Misery loves company"* and there is nowhere that this is truer than in counseling. It is of utmost importance to know your counselor and his capabilities.

The counselor must guard against permitting the counselee to transfer an attachment to the counselor, which would be detrimental to the counseling process. The wise counselor must never answer such as "I know what you are going through," or "I understand your situation." All people are different with different temperaments, diverse cultural upbringings, and different educational levels. Since each person is different, each problem must be treated differently. Even if the counselor went through the same difficulties as the person now being counseled their reaction to the problem may have been different, so the person must be counseled from a biblical perspective rather than a personal perspective. The counselor must keep in mind that the method that worked for one counselee may not work for another.

In the following chapter, we will look at the ways and reasons for changing one's core beliefs and why that is so important. The premise upon which we stand for this is found in the Bible and it goes something like, *"As a man thinketh, so is he."* in other words, we are what we think we are.

In chapter three, we shall discuss some of the dangers inherent in counseling. Unless we understand these dangers and guard against them, it would be easy to fall into the snare that the devil would set for those involved in this magnificent work. So, beloved, always be on your guard!

Changing One's Core Belief

I have found over the many years of counseling, that if a counselee is going to change his/her life to be an overcomer, rather than a victim, he must first change what he believes. A person's belief system, (what he believes about himself and life in general, what he believes about the difficulties he faces or is facing), will determine what he thinks, his thinking will determine his attitude, and his attitude will determine his behavior. Let me put it this way – If a person believes he is going to have something bad happen (an accident, a bad day), he will have that on his mind throughout the day, as a result, he will have a bad attitude about the little things, and that attitude will determine his conduct so that when something does happen, the first thing he will say is, "I knew it" or "I knew it was not going to be a good day." What is needed is for someone to come alongside and encourage the person to keep cheerful despite the awful situation and even in the troubled times something good can come out of it. The good counselor will not say he has the answer but rather ask, How can I help?

I had the privilege of counseling a family, (more than one, but I am thinking of one in particular), in one of the churches where I pastored. There seemed to be a constant barrage of allegations flying one way or another but finally, the wife said, "You have been a wonderful counselor and have helped us greatly." I patted myself on the back after they left the office, thinking that I had helped another family. However, it was not long before the husband stormed into my office telling me they were leaving the church. It was not my fault but the fault of the church because all the years they had been at the church they had constant trouble in the home.

I tried to talk with the man but he was determined not to listen to anything I said. He was not going to take responsibility for his home or his children. He was not home long enough to *"train up the children in the way that they should go"* (Proverbs 22:6). His poor wife was left with that responsibility. I believe that had the man given me time to talk with him, we could have gotten to the main issue, which was his core belief. He believed the church was the problem and he was not willing to talk with anyone, nor was he willing to change his belief about the church. He simply moved his family to another church and took the same baggage with him. I later discovered that he still had the same problems. If that man had been willing to come with his dear wife, I still believe the issue that bothered him could have been dealt with and restoration taken place. He would not, so it did not, and he did not receive restoration in his family or spiritual life.

Therefore, all counseling, to be successful, must keep Jesus Christ as the focus, and the attention of the counselee must be turned from himself and his problems toward the solution of the problem. In short, the counselee's core belief system needs to change. I passionately believe that if the counselee comes to counseling with an open mind and a willingness to work with the counselor permanent results will be accomplished.

I remember one person whom I counseled for several weeks who seemed to begin getting his life back together and was doing extremely well except in one area of his life that he was not willing to relinquish. His mind was completely focused on one thing. He got his anger under control and all but gave up drinking. He began to get his business plans in order so that he could work for himself and hire his own workers – that was all good. However, he did not want to hear about Jesus Christ, and what He could do for him if he would surrender to His Lordship.

After several weeks, and he was feeling much better, all he then wanted to talk about was sex. He was not willing to change his view of himself or those with whom he had contact, especially concerning his sexual promiscuity. I tried to get him to see that unless he began to focus on Jesus Christ and give Him first place, he would slip back to where he was before counseling, and maybe worse. He refused and spurned the grace of God until one day I had to let him know that I could no longer continue counseling him but that if at any time he felt that he needed someone to talk with I would still come to him. He has never called.

I have wondered many times about him and what I could have done differently to win him to Jesus. I still do not know the answer to that, and I fully realize that some cases must be left to the Lord.

The Bible states, *"As a man thinketh in his heart, so is he: ..."* Proverbs 23:7. In other words, 'a person is what he thinks he is.' Thus, if a person thinks that he is an addict, he is! My problem with 'AA,' 'NA,' and other twelve-step programs is that they constantly emphasize to the addict that they will always be an addict. The person may be in recovery for the next fifty years but they are still an addict. I take exception to that because it keeps the person thinking that he/she *"is"* an addict.

I want that person to change his thinking from 'I *am* an addict,' to 'I *was* an addict.' I teach counselees to remind himself or herself that they are on a journey. They are not what they used to be (that is past), they are not where they are going (that is future), but they are moving ahead (that is present).

The challenge for the counselee is to change what he believes. The challenge for the counselor is to help the counselee change what he believes. Once the belief is changed, the thinking will also change. When the thinking is changed, the attitude will change and then the manifestation of the attitude or behavior will also change.

The attitude is the combination of presuppositions, beliefs, convictions, and opinions that make up one's habitual stance at any given time toward a subject, person, or act. In other words, it is a mindset that strongly influences behavior. Jay E. Adams tells us "In counseling, attitudes may be attacked and changed more directly than feelings, which in most cases can be altered only indirectly through change of attitude and action or behavior."

Once the counselor has established a change in the thinking pattern of his counselee, he will then see a change in attitude. That change in attitude will result in a change of conduct.

What is behavior? It is responsible conduct. The term is best used to describe those activities of the whole person who may be judged by the law of God. There will not be a behavior change unless there is first an attitude change.

The Christian counselor should not at any time try to change a counselee's attitude or behavior. He must work at changing the counselee's core belief system because that belief system is what determines attitude, and the attitude will determine the behavior. Out of the hundreds of counseling cases I have had the privilege of helping, I have not had one problem person, but I have had hundreds of persons with problems. Whenever we see people with problems (mentally unhealthy or emotional), we can be assured that in most cases there will be an unhealthy belief system.

That unhealthy belief system must be changed, but the counselor must ever be cautious of the language, (both spoken and portrayed through body movements), used. Jay E. Adams says, "Language is a characteristic of God. God spoke and creation took place. Language can be determinative; it can spell the difference between success and failure in counseling. It is with language that we think as well as talk. The language was given to man alone at creation and plays a large part in making man unique among God's creatures. By language, people are capable of sustaining meaningful relationships with God and others. It made organized, interpretive thought possible."

The counselor must remember, at all times, that he must also be careful not to hurt the counselee's feelings while trying to help him change his belief system. This calls for a fine balancing act. The *"field is ripe unto harvest but the laborers are few"* (John 4:35). People are hurting and being hurt. They are discouraged, depressed, and oppressed, and they need someone to whom they can turn for help, someone who will not betray their confidence, and someone willing to listen and offer suggestions.

There will be periods of disappointment in counseling but the joy, happiness, satisfaction, and fulfillment in helping others become fruitful and live productive, victorious lives far outweigh any disappointment the counselor experiences. It is such a blessing to allow the Lord to work through you to help others overcome the battles of life.

The principles of counseling always remain the same, but the techniques will differ with different counselees. The technique employed to help one counselee change his core belief with remarkable success may be a dismal failure with another. The counselor must not force a technique just because it seems to be working. It may be that the counselor will have to change his technique in the middle of his counseling with the same counselee. No one wants to lose a counselee, but it does occasionally happen. In those times, the counselor should not become discouraged because the person he has helped in the past may be helping someone else and the multiplication of his counseling ministry has begun. *"With God, all things are possible. Only believe"* (Matthew 19:26; Mark 9:23; 10:27).

For effective counseling to take place, the counselor must have a heart of compassion, without which the counselor needs to get out of the field of counseling, do more studies, pray, and get the mind of the Holy Spirit before attempting such an important work. The counselee can easily see through the façade of someone who is just counseling for a paycheck. Beloved, counsel for the cause of Christ and you will receive satisfaction in knowing that you were instrumental in helping a hurting person carry their burden to the Lord.

Let me repeat: Change a person's core belief system and you will change an attitude, change behavior, and change the world, one soul at a time.

Dangers in Counseling

I would be remiss if I did not say that the person seeking counsel must understand that there are certain inherent dangers in seeking counseling. A great illustration is that of a person wishing to build a house. There are inherent dangers in the process when considering the various contractors for the job. Have they built houses for any length of time (Experience)? Are they licensed by the proper authorities? What is their record of accomplishment? And so forth.

II Corinthians 10:12 says, *"For we dare not make ourselves of the number, or compare ourselves with some that commend themselves: but they measuring themselves by themselves, and comparing themselves among themselves, are not wise."*

I have listed seven (there may be more) of the dangers that may be involved when a counselee is looking for a counselor:

1] The counselee may be simply looking for a rubber stamp of approval, rather than a genuine answer to the situation.

2] The counselee may have selective hearing. That is, he may not hear what he is being told but only what he wants to hear.

3] He may turn to the wrong kind of counselor. Is the counselor a psychologist, a children's counselor, a school counselor, and so forth?

4] The problem may not be correctly identified. Note, that if the counselee goes to the wrong counselor the problem may not be identified correctly, which could cause more difficulties for the counselee.

5] The counselee may have waited too long to seek help. Medical help may be needed rather than counseling.

6] The counselee may be seeking help from too many sources, which could bring about confusion.

7] The counselee may be simply looking for an answer to the problem, rather than finding biblical solutions.

Becoming a great professional counselor

Just as there are dangers for the counselee in seeking counseling, there are also dangers for the counselor he chooses, some of which will be listed under this heading.

The goal of every counselor, whether Christian or otherwise, I would hope, is to become the best possible counselor, by studying, consulting other counselors, and so forth. There are some things that the counselor must do if he is going to be a great counselor. First, he must put on godly virtues – that is, he must live a consistent Christian life according to the precepts of the Word of God. Second, he must put on love – that is, he must let the agape of God flow through him. He must have a passion for the Lord and compassion for people. Third, he must let the peace of God dwell in his heart. In other words, he must not let frustration or annoyance toward the counselee show. Fourth, the counselor must at all times have a heart of gratitude to the Lord for His many blessings. <u>Fifth</u>, the counselor must let the Word of God dwell in him richly. The better the counselor knows the Word, the more effective he will be as a counselor.

The Christian counselor must attain the highest professional ethics. He must be aware of this and accept complete responsibility for his ethical behavior. Moral judgments and moral attitudes are essential in the field of counseling. If one ignores his professional ethics, it will be to his peril. This, of course, runs directly into the necessity of confidential treatment of ALL information one is called upon to handle. No difficulty, no problem, must ever be looked at as just routine. The counselor must be careful that he does not handle any case with an 'I have heard all this before' attitude. If he does, he will have failed the counselee before ever getting to the root of the problem – where a solution can be found.

The counselor must remember that the reason the counselee is with him is because he is a trusted person and he must not betray that trust. The counselee is seeking to understand the basic principles of his life. The counselor, in turn, will have some of the necessary answers. Thus, he will have the necessary wisdom, and the counselee expects that their problem will be guarded with the greatest of discretion. The counselee should always be informed that the counselor is the only person with access to what has been shared with him. One of the first things I do when a counselee comes to me is to assure them of confidentiality. Also, in my case that confidentiality is doubled because I am first, an ordained minister of the Gospel of Jesus Christ, and, secondly, I am a licensed professional counselor.

Therefore, professional ethics are essential to all counsel; it will make the difference between success and failure. The professional Christian counselor must at all times recognize his limitations. People's problems are profoundly serious; they have to be dealt with seriously, and they have to be handled in the finest professional manner. This area of high ethical standards cannot be overemphasized.

Dr. Clyde Narramore says of professional ethics, "All one's 'know-how' and techniques amount to little if he is not careful about his counseling ethics. Ethical standards are essential to all counseling. They are too important to overlook or ignore." How true!

In addition to what I have already stated about professional ethics, Dr. Narramore suggests several other important matters concerning the counselor. I think it would be beneficial to enumerate some of those areas:

> 1] Never let the counselee see the notes you have made on his case.
>
> 2] Never use present case material as illustrations when speaking publicly, and especially do not reveal that the source for an illustration stems from counseling.
>
> 3] The counselor must never talk about other counselors.

4] The counselor must never discuss others with whom he has counseled or is presently counseling.

5] A wise counselor will never touch the counselee unnecessarily, except to shake hands, especially one of the opposite sex. How often has a good counselor, teacher, or minister been slandered and their ministry destroyed by such? God help us to be wise as serpents and harmless as doves!

6] The counselor must be careful about counseling in an appropriate place. A wise counselor avoids counseling in places like a parked car or a secluded area.

7] The counselor should never counsel someone of the opposite sex unless he leaves the office door ajar or has someone else in the counseling room with him.

8] At all times, the counselor and the counselee must be comfortable with each other. If there is discomfort during the counseling session, little will be accomplished in the counseling room.

9] Finally, both the counselor and the counselee must be protected from the appearance of impropriety.

All of these dangers can be overcome if the counselee does his homework in looking for the counselor who can best help him. In addition, the counselor must, when contacted by a potential counselee, investigate all possible avenues of helping the counselee accomplish his goal of getting better before accepting the counselee as a client. These things will help to avoid the many pitfalls for both the counselor and the counselee.

Just a little while ago, we received news that another pastor's wife was accused of inappropriate conduct because she was found in a car counseling a young man late at night. She denied the allegation, but it took its toll on the family and the ministry. This couple has since been able to overcome this traumatic experience but how much better it would have been if the lady had applied Biblical ethics.

Blessed is the counselor who uses wisdom when called upon to offer counseling to a hurting person.

Who is a Counselor?

A counselor is one who gives counsel or advises (Proverbs 11:14). In the Old Testament, the counselor was most often referred to as the king's advisor (II Samuel 15:12; I Chronicles 27:33), or one of the chief men of the government (Job 3:14; Isaiah 1:26). In Mark 15:43 and Luke 23:50 the word 'counselor' designated a "council member" of the Sanhedrin. In the Revised Standard Version of the Bible, the Holy Spirit is called *"The Counselor"* in John 14:16, 26; 15:26; 16:7. Isaiah 9:6 prophesies that Jesus Christ (Messiah) would be a wonderful Counselor.

Webster's Dictionary says that to counsel is to give advice, advise, or recommend a course of action. Thus, a counselor advises on a particular course of action. Such would be a lawyer, psychologist, psychiatrist, or Christian Counselor.

The New Concise Bible Dictionary says that a counselor is "one who gives advice, used of the Messiah in Isaiah 9:6, *"... and his name shall be called Wonderful, Counselor, The mighty God, The everlasting Father, The Prince of Peace,"* and the Holy Spirit in John 14:16, 26; 15:26; and 16:7. The Greek word has entered Christian thought as 'paraclete', and it means one who is called to stand by someone, especially in a law-court, hence the translation as 'advocate.' The help of the Spirit is seen in such legal terms in Matthew 10:19f, where Christians are envisaged as being on trial before secular and Jewish authorities."

The actual Greek word *"helein"* means to talk things over to plan or decide something; to seek an opinion from; to ask the advice of, to refer to, or turn to, especially for information; to keep in mind while acting or deciding to show regard for.

Baron–Byrne and Kantowitz, in their book "Psychology, Understanding Behavior" says that "counseling or counselors specialize in helping individuals who are experiencing many types of personal difficulties – but who show no signs of mental disorders – to resolve their problems. For example, counseling psychologists might assist a recently retired person to live a useful life in his community. In addition, they also frequently advise individuals on the choice of jobs consistent with their abilities and interests, or they would assist in the many spiritual problems that face and confuse believers in the Lord Jesus Christ." Remember Proverbs 15:22, which says, *"Without counsel, purposes are disappointed: but in the multitude of counselors, they are established."*

One is not a counselor simply because he/she hangs out a shingle and advertises such. It takes many years of study, research, and practice to become a competent counselor. All true counseling points the counselee to the great Counselor, the Lord Jesus Christ. Christian counseling is not Christian counseling just because it is called such – it is Christian counseling because it is counseling that has as its aim the changing of the heart of the person with his Lord, thereby changing that person's conduct and behavior. A counselor who is truly Christian will not use the theories of Carl Jung,

Mowrer, Rogers, or Freud as the basis for his counseling. Rather, he will use the Word of God as his rule and the Holy Spirit as his guide to bring about the necessary change in the person's thinking and ultimately his life.

Dr. Rob Johnson teaches correctly that secular counseling focuses on the problem and the client. Christian counseling is grounded in the Bible. It helps a person embrace pain through his or her relationship with Jesus. The processes of counseling are the same but the motivation is different.

We often hear how badly a person behaved in a particular situation, but we seldom hear the reason for such behavior. The Bible says, *"As he (person) thinks in his heart, so is he,"* Proverbs 23:7. Thus, when someone's thinking is in a negative mode, that person will act the way that he thinks. Again, people do not think badly because they feel bad – they feel bad because they think badly. A counselee's behavior does not determine his thinking – his thinking determines his behavior. Feelings do not determine one's actions – one's actions determine one's feelings.

The counselor must get to the root of the problem before he can adequately help a counselee. One may think the behavior is the problem but that is not the case. Behavior is just a symptom of the problem within. (My doctor once told me that I had to stop developing symptoms. I simply told my good Doctor that once we found the root of my physical ailments and dealt with them, the symptoms would go away). Psychologists and psychiatrists would like to shift the blame for a person's behavior to someone or something else. That is to say, the environment in which someone grew up is considered the cause of that one drinking alcohol or using drugs. Of course, the Christian counselor must understand that the root of the problem is sin, not the environment or some other such thing. Thus, the Christian counselor must make the counselee aware of the sin problem, and that he must take responsibility for his own behavior, and then point him to the One who can change his life, Jesus Christ.

Aspects of Counseling

There are many and varied aspects of counseling that one will face both in pastoral ministry and in counseling ministry. We shall look at some of these as we go through this writing. The counselor must always see his role as facilitating the Holy Spirit to do His work. If the counselor is going to be successful, he must pray before each session that the Holy Spirit will guide him in the proper direction, and he must never look at his position as a job. He participates in the ministry of helping hurting people. In other words, it might be said that he is a "therapon."

Language

I realize that I quoted Jay E. Adams in Chapter Two, about language, but I believe it bears repeating here.

As a counselor, one must be ever cautious of his/her language, (both spoken and portrayed through body movements), used. Jay E. Adams says, "Language is a characteristic of God. God spoke and creation took place. By the word of Satan man sinned. By the living and written Word of God man is saved." I will add to Dr. Jay Adams's thought to say that when Satan spoke to Eve in the Garden, he was deceptive and lying about the goodness of God – took the fruit and ate it. Out of her deception, she then gave it to Adam, who listened to the lie and ate the forbidden fruit – sin entered, and man found himself in a predicament that he could not extricate himself from. God stepped in and brought salvation to the world.

Dr. Clyde Narramore wrote, "When God created Adam and Eve, He gave them the power of speech, and ever since, people have spent much of their time talking." He continues with, "Language is an outlet for human expression. Talking is thinking; talking is sifting; talking is clarifying; talking is release, and talking is therapy." With this in mind, we can confidently say that talking has tremendous value. It is only through discussion that the counselee will be able to think and clarify his problem enough to find the solution to that problem.

Proverbs 18:20 points out that we feed ourselves, (not only others), on the words that we speak. *"A man's belly shall be satisfied with the fruit of his mouth; and with the increase* (produce) *of his lips shall he be filled. Death and life are in the power of the tongue: and they that love it shall eat the fruit thereof."* Therefore, we must always be mindful of the words we speak, whether positive or negative, for we will either be condemned or justified by our words (Matthew 12:37). Not only so, but every word or gesture that the counselor says/makes will have an effect on the counselee either for good or for bad. Thus, the counselor must not only be careful about what he speaks but how or what tone he uses when speaking.

As a child, I remember hearing an old saying something like this: "Sticks and stones may break my bones, but names or words will never hurt me." As children, we did not know how untrue that statement was. The bruising that comes from a stick or stone is physical and given time will heal. However, the words that we speak can destroy a person's ambition, goals, self-esteem, and so forth

---

sending that person into depression. Sometimes that hurt can go so deep as to send the person into fits of rage, and even lead to suicidal tendencies.

I know of one person who grew up in a "Christian home," but his dad would forever tell him how stupid he was. As the story goes, this man does not recall many times when his father told him he loved him. He was never told that he was bright or smart in given areas. It would be embarrassing to write the words used to describe how stupid this father indicated his son was. As a result, the son for many years hated his father and could not wait to get away from home. At a very young age, the young man feeling that he could not take more of the abusive language left home and went away to work.

Those words of baggage hung around the young man's neck like a noose, filling him with rage every time he thought of his father. Then one day a thought exploded in his mind. The light went on and the following thoughts ran through his mind, "I am not stupid. I may not be smarter than others, but I am just as smart. I may not be able to do what you can do but neither can you do what I can do. There is no such thing as a stupid person – some people may not have had opportunities to advance in certain areas, but they have taken advantage of what they have been offered and become great at what they do. Everyone starts at the same level and moves along as they are given opportunity, encouragement, and funds." That young man then decided to turn his life around, to become the highest educated person in that large family. He started to study with the wrong motive but he started anyway and earned certificates as a Private Investigator. He learned how to perform stakeouts, take a person's fingerprints, and read them, among other things. He accepted Jesus Christ as his Savior and then earned his first theological degree, after which his motive changed, and he continued to study because he loved to learn. He was one of the fortunate ones who learned with time to overcome rather than be a victim. Words almost cost that young man his life as he often thought it would be better to commit suicide and get it over.

That man developed a slogan for himself which he has taught to hundreds of counselees to help them pull out of the trap the enemy has them in. That slogan is, 'I can do anything I want to do. How bad do I want it?' The Bible says, *"I can do all things through Christ who strengthens me,"* Philippians 4:13.

The counselor will also have to deal with different people's feelings. Even though he wants to help the counselee, by all means possible, he must be extremely cautious not to offend the counselee with the words that are spoken or the body language. Dealing with the feelings of the counselee refers primarily to the perception by the counselee of a bodily state as pleasant or unpleasant. Proverbs 18:19 indicates it is quite difficult to win the trust of the counselee once it has been broken saying, *"A brother offended is harder to be won than a strong city: and their contentions are like the bars of a castle."*

Attitude

In this vital ministry of counseling, the counselor will also have to contend with the problems of attitude expressed by the counselee. Attitude is the combination of presuppositions, beliefs, convictions, and opinions that make-up one's habitual stance at any given time toward a subject, person, or act. Attitude is a mindset that strongly influences behavior. In actuality, a person's feelings determine his attitude, and his attitude determines his behavior or conduct. By way of illustration, let me relate to you a brief story: A young child was badly misbehaving when the company was visiting the home. It seemed that regardless of what was tried the child continued to misbehave. Eventually, the final warning was given, and the child was told to sit on a certain chair and remain there until permission was granted for him to move. The boy sat for a few moments and then announced, "I might be sitting on the outside, but I am still standing on the inside." That is attitude!

Dr. Clyde Narramore says, "In counseling, attitudes may be attacked and changed more directly than feelings, which in most cases can be altered only indirectly through a change of attitude and action or behavior." In other words, there will be no genuine change of attitude about something until a person changes his feelings about it.

Behavior is responsible conduct. The term is best used to describe those activities of the whole person who may be judged by the law of God. There will not be a behavior change until there is an attitude change. A person's attitude determines his behavior.

The Christian counselor may be involved in generalized counseling practices much the same as a pastor, or he may do specialized counseling. Generalized counseling will involve a range of counseling for children, youth, or seniors, and include such areas as loss of loved ones (bereavement), sexual problems (including homosexuality, lesbianism, and other perversions or deviant sexual behavior), marital and family problems, just to name a few. Specialized areas of counseling may include what I was doing before being disabled, which was addiction counseling. My practice included various addictions such as alcohol, drugs, and so forth. I knew of another counselor who specialized in sexual counseling. Nonetheless, in all cases of counseling, whether generalized or specialized, the goal is to get the counselee to change their belief about the problem, which will help them change their attitude, which leads to a change in their behavior (responsible conduct) by pointing them to Christ, the Great Counselor.

The Christian counselor need not be reminded that he has been called to labor in opposition to the world, the flesh, and the devil. His task involves not merely a struggle with flesh and blood, but also a fight against the supernatural forces of darkness. Ephesians 6:12 put it this way, *"For we wrestle not against flesh and blood, but against principalities, against powers, against the rulers of the darkness of this world* (age), *against spiritual wickedness* (spiritual hosts of wickedness, wicked spirits) *in heavenly* (high) *places."*

Therefore, effective counseling must be understood and conducted as a spiritual battle. Hence, there is a need for divine authority in counseling, and only Biblical counseling possesses such authority. The Christian counselor should exercise the full authority for the counseling that Christ gave to the organized church. First Thessalonians 5:12-14 says, *"And we beseech you, brethren, to know* (recognize) *them who labor among you, and are over you in the Lord, and admonish* (instruct, counsel) *you;* 13) *and to esteem them very highly in love for their work's sake. And be at peace among yourselves.* 14) *Now we exhort* (counsel) *you, brethren, warn them that are unruly* (insubordinate)*, encourage the faint-hearted, support the weak, be patient toward all men."* Thus, the counselor must consider himself a soldier of Christ engaged in spiritual warfare when counseling. For this battle, the *"full armor of God"* alone is sufficient. That armor is found in Ephesians 6.

When I first began to preach about demonic influence and how to live free in Christ one person came to me and said, "Pastor, I do not think that is a good thing to talk about in a public service. I do not want the children exposed to something that may take place." What that person did not understand is that God is not in the business of frightening people and there does not have to be some outstanding manifestation-taking place for God's people to be set free. All the Lord asks for is honest hearts that want to serve Him in spirit and in truth for *"he whom the Son sets free is free indeed."*

That person was bound by fear of the unknown and did not realize it. Rather than seek release from the bondage of fear, the family chose to worship elsewhere. I have since discovered the reason for this unfounded fear was that various persons had in the past, gone to the extreme with the teaching on deliverance. It seemed that they saw demons under every rock, which is unscriptural. Most people can be set free from the hurts of life with a little godly counseling and understanding.

Techniques for effective
Counseling

Webster's dictionary describes "technique" as a 'technical procedure or method of doing something.'

Another dictionary defines "technique" as a method of performance, a way of accomplishing.

In counseling, different techniques (procedures, methods) must be employed for different people. In other words, not all counseling is the same. The counselor would do well to remember that if he tries to use the same technique or method for each counselee, he may have enormous success with one counselee but be a miserable failure with another. Two people may have the same problem but two completely separate ways of looking at the problem; therefore, a different technique must be used in the counseling process for these persons. The counselor must never be afraid to change his style or method of counseling with individuals as this could mean the difference between success and failure.

Effective counseling means having the compassion of Christ and going that extra mile to help a hurting person. All ministries will involve a certain amount of counseling, whether it is teaching a Sunday school class, leading youth services, street ministry, visitation, and so forth. To do effective counseling we need the power of the Holy Spirit, the love of God, and the aforementioned compassion of Jesus Christ. Quite often, my clients would ask me how I could keep smiling when I had to deal with so much from them. The answer was always quite simple. I love my Lord and have given everything to Him; therefore, I am relaxed in my ministry to each individual. A counselor must never try to force anything during the counseling process. Rather, he should relax, let the counselee talk, and wait upon the blessed Holy Spirit to give direction for the counseling session.

I will never forget when I asked one of my counselees to leave the building for failure to abide by the rules. (You see, I had an average of fourteen to nineteen clients living together for a six to nine-month counseling program to get them free from various drugs, alcohol, and gambling). Our policy was that if they fell off the wagon, so to speak, for the third time, or their attitude did not change and they were creating a disturbance for the rest of the group, they were asked to leave the program and the building. It was an uncomfortable and contradictory position to be in, as a minister. On the one hand, I was telling them that God loved them and that I also cared for them, while on the other hand, I had to ask them to leave the building because they had gone back to their old lifestyle or they were a threat to other clients and possibly staff members.

One day after giving the final warning, I asked one man to leave. He said "ok" and went to his room. Another counselor was sitting with me in the office when suddenly it sounded like the man was demolishing everything. Various things were being thrown against the wall while he kept screaming and cursing. My helper stood up to go to him but I cautioned him to stay where he was and let the man calm down. Eventually, the man calmed down and came to my office in a very repentant mood asking to be permitted to stay. Again, I had to inform him that he must leave but that I would help him in any way I could. He packed his belongings, and I helped him move them out. Several days later, that man came to see me and to let me know that he was now doing very well. I discovered that he had bad feelings because of the way he was raised so he developed a bad attitude and showed it through his behavior. All the while dealing with this person, I kept a calm, cool, but firm attitude with a smile on my face and he understood that I was not judging him. I wanted to help him. I realized that it would take more than mere counseling with him because he had several mental deficiencies, which needed medical attention. When we contacted the Doctor and other health professionals, including the police and the courts, they were willing to help him based on my reputation and recommendation to the system. Again, I repeat, each counselee may of necessity be treated with different techniques and if one does not seem to be working, the counselor should not be afraid to try another.

Professional Growth and
The Wise Counselor

Earlier, I briefly mentioned professional ethics, but here I would like to state that even with this type of knowledge, there is still a continual need for professional growth. It is important for all counselors to continually be involved in further courses of study, or the purchase of more up-to-date counseling material, to keep in step with any new methods and approaches there might be in counseling. If a counselor feels at any time that he has gone as far as he can, he should refrain from the counseling field because he will find himself in trouble quite quickly.

Dr. Hambly, the Chairperson of the Evangelical Order of Certified Pastoral Counselors of America, (E.O.C.P.C.A), tells the following story concerning himself, and I quote: "I had written twelve papers concerning the Gospel of John plus a final exam. My professor sent my paper back with the word, "Excellent"! My ego burst forth, and then on the last page he had written, 'You have just scratched the surface.' I was extremely angry, felt insulted, and now I realize after all these years that he was right in his assessment."

Just as a baby needs milk to grow, so the professional counselor needs certain things to continue growth in his chosen field. The counselor needs to attend lectures, read good books, seek the best material for perusal, and continue to address his progress at every opportunity. The true mark of a professional is his desire to improve his understanding of his chosen field in the most detailed manner. The true professional will endeavor to broaden his horizons regardless of the cost. In addition to the above, he will take as many courses as possible, especially on professional subjects. Time and money should never be a factor in advancing one's knowledge as a professional counselor.

A few days ago, I went to see my doctor. It seems that I have a particular disease, (non-contagious), that is rare but will never kill me. However, everything that I found out about this disease says there is an amount of pain associated with it. My doctor went immediately to his medical book to read up on the subject – that is a professional! It is not a matter of having a certain number of books in the library, but how many of the books have you read? It may be that rather than buying more books we need to read or re-read the ones we already have. Personal, and professional growth is the key to being the best we can be in any chosen field of endeavor - especially counseling. The E.O.C.P.C. tells us that we have to read at least one new book on counseling each year to retain our licensure as certified counselors.

Daily, the counselor will be confronted with new methods, innovative ideas, and novel approaches, so he must never feel there is nothing more to learn. Counseling is a science, so we can gain much insight from those who have devoted their life to it, even from secular counselors and psychologists.

As professional counselors, we must remember that we are not masters of every subject we have to deal with. We must also remember that at the root of every problem lay one word – SIN. Marital break-ups, unfaithfulness, alcoholism, abuse, mental illness, behavior disorders, homosexuality, and so forth. Truly, the need is great, and although we may not have the necessary inner depth of knowledge for every area, we should at least study enough to have a basic understanding to know which direction to point the counselee.

The wise counselor will seek to be as knowledgeable as possible in all areas of counseling. He will also understand there may be cases that require someone with more in-depth knowledge in a particular area than he has. It is never a failure to admit that one is not equipped for a particular case. At such a point, it is wise to suggest someone else. I have had cases that needed medical attention and knowing my limitations, I have sent them to see a family doctor who diagnosed their condition and gave proper medication to aid the patient in recovery.

Some time ago, a murder took place in our area, and it involved the family of a particular church. My wife and I had attended that church for about two years and the pastor was a young, dynamic, preacher. He holds a Master of Divinity degree from a much-respected University and is the Chaplin for the military base in our city. However, when this tragedy occurred, this wonderful man of God sought someone else to counsel the family. In his words, "I am not qualified to counsel this type of situation." All church leaders should have the capability to counsel in all cases but unfortunately, they do not. Every believer can counsel in certain situations but not in all situations and it is a wise counselor who recognizes his limited ability.

Early in 2008, I was invited to be part of the ministerial staff of a certain church in another part of Canada. I was told that the pastor was not equipped to counsel his people so they needed a licensed counselor on staff who could perform that function. That is the very reason that psychologists and psychiatrists have taken the counseling role away from pastors while the pastor sits idly by watching his people go to ungodly people to receive counseling. What a shame! It is time for Bible College, Universities, and other training institutions to teach Christian counseling as part of their study program. If it were a requirement, I do not believe pastors and teachers would go through such drama and burnout when serious problems are encountered, whether inside or outside the classroom.

The trained, who is wise, will endeavor to know as much about the law as possible in the area where he works as a counselor. He should talk with social workers, lawyers, probation officers, Children's Aid, and other professionals who can offer assistance. He will also spend time in a courtroom to learn what happens in that environment. In essence, he will be as fully informed about the climate of his community as possible.

This writer has spent many hours in the courtroom witnessing on behalf of clients who would become my counselees. I have spent time talking with the defense attorneys and the prosecution attorneys. I have spent days in the correctional facility talking with inmates who would eventually be my counselees. Both the judges and the prosecutors have come to know me and within two years, I won about ninety-nine percent of the cases I fought for. It became a joy for me to sit in the witness box and tell the entire courtroom that what those addicts needed was an encounter with Jesus Christ. The only way they would get free of the bondage that held them to stay clean and live productive lives in society was to surrender their life completely to the lordship of the Savior. One such judge asked me if a person who is not of the Judeo-Christian faith would be permitted into my program. I was happy to tell the judge and the entire courtroom audience that I would accept anyone of any background – faith or no faith, but unless that person accepted the cleansing of the Savior, I did not doubt that he would go back to the pigpen of his addictions again. Programs are good but what is needed is deliverance by the blood and Spirit of Jesus Christ. The wise counselor will go to battle for his counselees. He will fight the works of the devil (1 John 3:8; cf. John 10:10) and point that soul to the greatest of all Counselor – Jesus, the Lamb of God.

One of my counselees was a gay person. He informed me that God made him that way, so he could not help it. I had the opportunity to study the subject sometime earlier but decided to take a fast refresher course from the resources in my library and see what the Bible said about the subject, in both Old and New Testaments. The next time my counselee came to see me, I took him through the Old Testament and then into the New Testament to show him God's view of homosexuality. Then I asked him, 'Do you think that God would create you as a homosexual and then say that the sin of homosexuality was an abomination to Him?' He, being confronted with the issue had to admit that it was indeed wrong and a sin that needed to be repented of. The sad thing is that when faced with this, he decided to walk away, just as the rich young man walked away from the Lord in Matthew 19:16-22. As a wise counselor, I could not condemn the man but point him to the Savior and then pray for him.

Counseling the Mentally and Emotionally ill

In this chapter and the next, I want to highlight just two areas of counseling that the counselor will have to face in his practice. Both of these areas seem to raise their ugly head whether one is involved in addictions counseling, marriage counseling, family counseling, or counseling the youth and so forth. These two are: 1) The mentally & emotionally ill, and 2) Sexual Problems.

Some time ago, an article appeared in the P. E. I. Guardian concerning depression. Depression affects a person both mentally and emotionally. There were not a lot of new things in the article except for recent figures, which should make us aware of the illness faced in this area. (There is no doubt that the figures would have changed since the writing of this manuscript). The article stated that the yearly bill to employers (in Canada) for long-term disabilities has reached three hundred million dollars a year, which covers about 670,000 workers.

Those figures are but a fraction of the toll that is taken because of depression. As great as the numbers would be for depression, most of it remains hidden because people do not always recognize the signs. The signs are many, and some that the wise counselor should take time to familiarize himself with are:

1] The inability to concentrate and make decisive decisions

2] Decreased productivity.

3] An unusual increase in errors and a decline in dependability.

4] Frequent tardiness and too many sick days.

5] Irritability, and in some cases, hostility.

6] Alcohol and/or drug abuse.

I have found that almost all of the counselees who have come to me for alcohol and drug abuse counseling have been severely depressed. Many cases have had poor concentration and great irritability. Most of those people feel poorly about themselves and think everyone else sees them the same way they see themselves. Whenever this has been detected, I have sent them to a medical doctor for diagnosis before beginning counseling for the addictions.

We must remember that "depression is not a weakness; it is an actual sickness which can be treated in most cases," (Canadian Mental Health Association).

Collins Dictionary (Canadian Edition) says when a person is depressed, he feels "hollow, low in spirits, dejection, despondency, slump."

Webster's gives a fuller understanding of the word. It says depression is "the state of being or the act of depressing; a condition of deep dejection characterized by a lack of response to stimulation and withdrawal."

Thank God, we have advanced in recognizing the importance of knowing the role played in our emotional understanding of the absolutes that influence our bodily health. As to our psychosomatic, (Psyche – Mind; Somo – Body), health there are numerous books available to help us. Unfortunately, there is still misunderstanding concerning the whole person and the needed treatment but counselors need to equip themselves as much as possible in every area.

Whenever there are emotional problems, the objective should be to deal, as quickly as possible, with the emotional conflict. Emotional conflicts will eventually lead to physical illnesses if not dealt with. It is sad that in most cases, the counselor does not see the counselee until after visible physical needs appear. I believe that if the emotional problems are dealt with promptly, the symptoms of physical illness may be prevented from showing up, or, if they have shown up, they will disappear rather quickly. The counselor must remember that dealing with emotional factors takes time and skill.

The Bible is emphatic when it says, *"Therefore, my beloved, as you have always obeyed, not as in my presence only, but now much more in my absence, work out your own salvation with fear and trembling.* 13) *For it is God who works in you both to will and to do of his good pleasure,"* Philippians 2:12-13.

Learning how to handle emotions will lessen the cause and effect. Reaching a better understanding of things common to us will not allow us to fall prey to the illness, which usually accompanies the action. This is an area in which preventative medicine may be practiced. The practicing counselor should be extremely sensitive to the counselee in helping him/her to overcome the painful past, thus releasing some of the emotional tensions. People who have had troubled, unhappy, lives require help. Not only do they need present guidance to emotional and spiritual health but the continual acceptance of them back into community life, will make a complete difference.

There is one thing, that if impressed upon the counselee's mind, may minimize their problem, and that is their trusting in Christ daily. The greatest comfort is God's comfort; He is all love and mercy. The Christian counselor is the person who is more often in a position to be helpful to people who find themselves in emotional distress. However, he must always remember that he cannot rush the counselee – he must be patient, (longsuffering), loving and kind, and ever listening to the counselee without being judgmental.

In the following chapter, we will deal with counseling the sexually troubled person.

Counseling those with
Sexual Problems

In 2005, I had the opportunity to sit in a class for eight hours of instruction on sexual problems, their consequences, and how to *counsel* those caught in the trap, given by Dr. Carnes of Mississippi, USA. At that time, we were told the statistics revealed that 60% of Canadian students did their homework while watching pornography on the internet. Recently, in the province where I reside in Canada, statistics revealed that only 14% of children using the internet are supervised and 70% of children gamble. It seems that it is very easy to do so when more than 2300 gambling and casino sites are available to them. In addition, when parents have to work two and sometimes three jobs just to meet their financial obligations, there is very little supervision for the children.

Add to this the growing number of students who are sexually active and we have a severe problem. Note that in early 2007 there was breaking news concerning another pornographic ring broken that involved some seventy-seven countries.

Dr. Carnes stated, "We are sitting on a powder keg that is about ready to explode." Most secularists, humanistic, counselors, psychologists, and psychiatrists do not seem to see a problem with young people being sexually active. The important thing is for them to be protected during their sexual promiscuity, so we are told. May God have mercy! They have taken God out of the school and put condoms in. They have taken the Bible and prayer out of our schools and we see the results in school shootings, rape, swarming, and so forth.

In February 2008, news broke that in one of our fine provinces in Canada, another swarming took place in which some twenty-five children between the ages of twelve and fifteen swarmed a nineteen-year-old female and her brother. Thus, we are raising children with no respect for parents, teachers, the law, or themselves. What a shame!

We need more Christian counselors trained, who are willing, ready, and able to take on the various problems associated with such widespread promiscuity. We need Christian counselors, who will be firm, yet compassionate; Counselors who will not condemn, yet, not condone; Counselors who will use the Word of God as their rulebook, and take the Holy Spirit as their Guide; Counselors, who will not judge the counselee, but rather gain an understanding of the forces at work in their lives. The wise counselor will never jump to conclusions but wait patiently for the real problem to begin to be revealed by the counselee.

Sexual problems grow out of the fact that SEX is a vital force in our lives. Self-control has to be one of the key phrases here, for it is only as we permit our urges to get out of control that we suffer the consequences, which are usually quite severe. Some of these are:

1. Sexual incompatibility

2. Habitual masturbation

3. Homosexuality

4. Fornication, resulting in an unexpected pregnancy

5. Sexually transmitted diseases (STDs)

This brief list indicates that personal freedom comes with a definite cost. In other words, freedom is not a license to do what one wishes to do without restraint. When one tries to live in freedom without restraint, chaos follows. Anyone who endeavors to live in promiscuity must expect to face instant, burning passions. These are normal for the majority of people with an uncontrolled sex drive.

God has granted strong attraction for different sexes, and the desire to love another. I try to impress upon counselees that most of the problems they face with falling in love come from what they believe about love. Love is not something that one falls into – love is a commitment. The desire that God has placed within men and women to cohabitate, that the population may constantly be replenished, has been turned into a lust to satisfy the sexual desire. Man has taken this natural desire and promoted it to the absolute extreme; he has covered every avenue, seeking to be the controller of that which is a God-given drive. We must see that this intense force is so directed as to honor God, to honor Him as He set it down in His Word. If one does not have his sexual drive under control in a God-honoring manner, one will have nothing but untold problems.

As counselors, we continually face unprecedented opposition to any control over one's body. Some time ago, in the city of Scarborough, Canada, separate classes were set up for Black students and young gay people. Of course, gay teachers are instructing young gay people. We now have early sex education, free condoms, and no shame in unwanted pregnancies, unrestricted access to abortion as there seems to be no need for any moral implication or direction. In Canada, the abortion law has been stuck down so that now an abortion can be performed at any time and for any excuse. In any society, when God and the Bible are taken out of the classroom, society degenerates into a hellish mess orchestrated by the devil. They can call it fun, excitement, or enjoying oneself if they want, but there will always be the aftermath of degradation and the inevitable price to pay.

Dr. Clyde Narramore tells us, "Sex is not confined to just one aspect of life. It extends to all of a person's being – intermingling with their emotions, their intellect, their physical attributes, and their spiritual development."

As a counselor, every time I have had to work with someone who has deviant sexual problems, I have found many accompanying problems. Those accompanying problems will generally have a direct bearing on the counselee's sexual difficulties. One partner may have a sexual over-drive while the other has an incredibly low sex drive and this incompatibility creates a myriad of additional problems, which many times end up in the divorce court. The answer to this dilemma is found only in surrendering one's life completely to the Lordship of Jesus Christ.

The counselor's work is to encourage professional help as soon as possible to stem the flow, teaching people to openly address their needs, endeavoring to understand each other's feelings, and understanding their own feelings. It is a distinct possibility that the counselor will end up being a substitute for the work, which should have been accomplished by the parents. It is also possible the counselor may end up introducing the counselee to a wholesome sexual education.

Increasingly we see the sexual bombardment by every phase of the media, which has aided our generation in developing unrealistic and unchristian attitudes toward sex. This ongoing bombardment has given many an attitude that can never be fully reached or realized. Thus, we have an unregenerate population and those who have been raised in so-called "good" homes also fall into the pit of Satanic-controlled activities. Society sees a sinful, degraded, generation as being normal. God help us!

Hollywood has glamorized sexual promiscuity (heterosexuality and homosexuality/lesbianism) so much so that if one takes a stand against this ungodliness, he is classed as homophobic. Turn the TV from one station to the next and all one sees is someone getting into bed with one person and then with someone else. During the Oscars, the Junos, and other award shows the women appear half-naked. Truly, we have become so desensitized to it that just about anything goes. What a shame!

Let me pose this two-fold question: 'What is the answer, and what can the Christian counselor do to deal with the various, deviant, sexual needs with which we are confronted daily? The answer is in a consecrated relationship with God. This is a sure safeguard against all types of deviation and perversion. The greatest asset in thwarting Satan's destructive plan is to see people get right with the Savior.

The Christian counselor first must make sure of his relationship with the Lord so that upon hearing the incredulous, heart-wrenching stories of various broken lives with which he deals, he will remain objective in the face of it all. If a counselor loses his objectivity, he will fail in his counseling practice and the person he is trying to help will not receive the help that he so desperately desires.

I have had to listen to stories of how a dad beat his son with a baseball bat continually when the son was only five years old. I have been told the stories of how a mother molested her son for several years until the son was filled with hatred and anger. There have been times when I felt like... but the grace of God kept me calm and peaceful as I heard these horrific stories. Had I let my humanity show during these times, I would not have been able to remain objective and help these counselees. These are the times when the counselor must rely upon the grace of God.

Freud vs. Jung vs. the Christian Counselor

I have already mentioned Freud, Mowrer, and Jung but throughout this thesis have endeavored to maintain a spiritual perspective. However, now I want to digress a little to look at some of the teachings of L. A. Pervin in his book "Personality, Theory Assessment, and Research." Pervin states, "Freud's psychoanalytic personality was the first to be discussed from the standpoint of theory, assessment, and research. It was the first model, so to speak, to exist.

"Psychoanalysis has as its main thrust in the interplay among forces in human behavior. Behavior is viewed as a multiplicity of complex problems among motives, drives, needs, and conflicts occurring at various levels of awareness. We are constantly changing and improving them." Pervin goes on to point out that, Freud said, "man was "lived" by unknown, unconscious and at times uncontrollable forces."

As brilliant as Freud was, he was still a man plagued by periods of depression all of his life and occasionally used cocaine to calm the stress and depressive moods that he experienced. Of his periods of depression he said, "My recovery can only come through work in the unconscious; I cannot manage with conscious efforts alone." How sad! If he had only realized that the answer to his struggles with depression was found in Jesus Christ, what a tremendous difference he may have had in society. Freud had a brilliant mind but chose to reject the one person who could help him fulfill his potential in life. That person is the Lord Jesus Christ.

Freud, like thousands of other scholars, was not able to "break out" into the realm of spirituality where freedom and truth abound. Thus, his genius was bound by unseen chains of darkness that prevented him from becoming the beautiful child of God that the heavenly Father intended him to become.

Freud was so close, yet so far away! However, one by-product of his investigations was that a whole series of men began to take personality and its peculiarities much more seriously than ever before. One such was Carl Jung, who was so impressed with Freud's work that he went to work with him for several years. He later departed due to a disagreement with Freud over Freud's insistence upon the identification of his method with his sex theory. Jung felt that Freud's theory of pansexualism was inadmissible. In Psychiatry Pansexualism pertains to the theory that all human behavior is based on sexuality. It also expresses sexuality in all its forms or involves sexual activity with people of any gender or with people regardless of their gender. (H'm, that sounds like the world in which we now live, don't you think)?

Jung's new method became known as analytical psychology. Jung is acknowledged to be one of the foremost psychological thinkers of the 20th century. He believed that man's behavior is conditioned not only by his individual and racial history (causability) but also by his aims and aspirations (teleology).

Both the past and the future guide one's present behavior. "The person lives by aims as well as by causes." This fact sets Jung apart from Freud. Freud felt that it was the belief in the endless repetition of instinctual themes until one dies. On the other hand, Jung felt that there is constant and often creative development. Jung says that modern humans have been molded by the cumulative experiences of past generations, while Freud says that man is what he is because of infantile origins.

Neither of these gentlemen put forth a position for the behavior of people in response to the Word of God and living a life based upon the cross of Christ. Neither of these seemed to believe that men need to take responsibility for their actions. Neither did they put forth a position that man is what he thinks he is (Proverbs 23:7) because he believes what he believes. As a man believes, so he thinks – his thinking then determines his attitude and his attitude determines his behavior or conduct. The Christian counselor, on the other hand, will encourage the counselee to take responsibility for his actions, (as painful as that may be, at times), and then point him to the burden-bearer, the life-changer, Jesus Christ. The one thing that the Christian counselor must never forget is that he can only counsel through the guidance of the Holy Spirit and he must always point the counselee to Jesus.

I recently told my class they would never be able to help someone unless they can get the person to change the way they believe. That is, unless one changes what he believes about himself, the difficulties he faces, and those around him and puts God into the equation, his life will never change.

The counselee must of necessity, be encouraged to change the focus of his/her thinking from the problem to the problem solver. However, I must interject here a cautionary note to the counselor that he cannot just use Jesus Christ as a fix-all or crutch upon which to lean in times of trouble. Jesus is not like a genie in a bottle and if we rub Him the right way or use the right words, He will jump out and do our bidding. NO!

The counselor must have a life that is consecrated to following the teaching of the Lord Jesus Christ.

Then, and only then, will he be able to point the counselee in the right direction. Even though the Christian counselor may, (of necessity), have to learn some of the thinking and techniques of the secular humanist, he must never use their methods and theories for counseling those who come to him for help. Rather, he must work within the confines of the Word of God and be led by the blessed Holy Spirit.

The Counselor's Position in Christ

In Matthew 6, we are made aware of how Jesus went all over the region of Galilee teaching in the Synagogues and preaching about the Kingdom of God, healing the sick, and casting out demons. Luke 4:14 tells us that when Jesus returned, from the wilderness after fasting and prayer with the Father, after his temptation by the devil, *"He was in the power of the Spirit."* Ezekiel 36:27 says, *"And I will put my Spirit within you..."* In Romans 8:9 the Apostle Paul writes, *"But ye are not in the flesh, but in the spirit, if so be that the Spirit of God dwells in you,"* and I Corinthians 3:16 he asks the question, *"Know ye not that ye are the temple of God, and that the Spirit of God dwelleth in you?*

We must remember the prophet Joel who spoke the word of God saying, *"And it shall come to pass afterward, that I will pour out my spirit upon all flesh; and your sons and your daughters shall prophesy, your old men shall dream dreams, your young men shall see visions.*" The Holy Spirit of God has a specific ministry for each of us to do, and so He empowers us to do service for the Lord Jesus Christ. In Acts 1:8, we are told, "*But you shall receive power after the Holy Spirit has come upon you: and you shall be witnesses unto me both in Jerusalem, and in all Judea, and in Samaria, and unto the uttermost part of the earth.*" Thus, the Christian counselor must never forget Hebrews 13:8, which says, "*Jesus Christ the same yesterday, and today and forever.*" The foregoing Scriptures open up for us an understanding of our position in Christ. Our position is one of power and authority because of the indwelling of the Holy Spirit. Personal relationship seems to be the key to our position in Christ, which extends to anger and how to deal with it. Jesus worked miracles, healed the sick, cast out demons, and so forth. We, as Christians (Christ followers), can do the works of our Savior because we have all of heaven standing with us. God "*has raised us up together, and made us sit together in heavenly places in Christ Jesus:*" Ephesians 2:6

The Bible tells us that our position in Christ will make us as cautious as snakes and as gentle as doves and that we will have to suffer many human indignities, but we are not to worry because the words that we speak will not be ours; they will come from the Spirit of our Father speaking in and through us - if we are living in the Spirit – (cf. Romans 8:9-11, 13-14). The Christian counselor's position in Christ is that his eyes see and his ears hear what the Spirit shows and tells us.

As counselors, we must come to the place where we see, hear, and understand, that Christ is truly the God the Son as much as He is the Son of God. If we do not, then no true spiritual counseling will take place. The counselee will have to go away disappointed once again with no living bread to eat. What a shame! For we, as Christian counselors, do have access to the storehouse of God. We should remember what the Bible teaches in Acts 11:24, *"For he* (Barnabas) *was a good man, and full of the Holy Spirit and of faith: and many people were added unto the Lord."* Thus, we must know our position in Christ, especially if we are going to be used as counselors in any sense of the word and it is only the Holy Spirit that can make any sense of the Word of God.

When the counselor is in the position of receiving the treasures of the Lord God, he will then know what it is he is being helped by God's Holy Spirit to accomplish with the counselee. How can the counselor "know" if he has never been there himself? So many psychiatrists, psychologists, social workers, and secular counselors in general, talk and learn theory, and by a sort of quasi-experimental basis, present a plan to a counselee that simply does not work in most cases. If these humanistic people would be truthful, they would tell you that one has to "keep trying" until a method "clicks." They call it diverse or eclectic psychological methodology. Sorry to say, but most counselees get lost and go away with their unresolved problem which then is compounded into excruciating mental anguish. This is needless and quite harmful! For the Lord tells us in Deuteronomy 28:15-67 what will happen if we fail to hear and heed His voice, 15] *"But it shall come to pass, if you will not hearken unto the voice of the LORD your God, to observe to do all his commandments and his statutes which I command you this day; that all these curses shall come upon you, and overtake you:* 16] *Cursed shall you be in the city, and cursed shall you be in the field.* 17] *Cursed shall be your basket and your kneading trough.* 18] *Cursed shall be the fruit of your body, and the fruit of your land, the increase of your cattle, and the offspring of your sheep.* 19] *Cursed shall you be when you come in, and cursed shall you be when you go out.* (One would do well to get the Bible and read the rest of the verses for oneself). Therefore, we can see the importance of preparation for the position of the high calling of the counselor in the Lord, our God. One may have this calling to be a Christian Counselor and be made to sit together with Christ in the heavenly places, but unless he is willing to spend the necessary time in preparation for this lofty ministry, God will not be able to use him. We also see the importance of being in constant fellowship and obedience to the Word and will of the Lord. The Word is our instruction Manual and the Holy Spirit is our guide.

When the counselor leads the counselee to realize and practice his relationship with the Lord, he will undoubtedly be in a position where he will give honor and glory to the name of Jesus Christ. The counselee will then be able to manage the blessings and challenges that God wants him/her to have. A natural by-product will be the defeat of Satan's hold over individuals! May God give us more Christ-centered counselors who are dedicated to the cause of Christ and the liberation of souls held in bondage by the enemy. The spiritual counselor must without sympathy for sin, have real compassion and love (empathy) for the sinner. When good fruit becomes part of the counselor's daily living, he will emerge as the kind of person in whom others will have confidence, and his counseling will prove effective.

Dealing with the Root
Rather than the Symptom

When I went to see my GP, (Doctor), to find out what was happening to my health, he sent me to the hospital for various tests such as ex-rays, CT scans, blood work, and so forth. At one point, he looked at me and said, *'You have to stop developing symptoms'* to which I replied that the symptom is not the problem - the root is the problem. We must discover the root and deal with that, then the symptoms will disappear. Since then, he has given me prescriptions to help with the symptom while he seeks to find the root through another battery of tests.

The same principle holds true in counseling. Alcohol and drug abuse is how the counselee copes with the hidden problem. Over many years of counseling, I have often looked at the counselee and told them that their drinking or excessive use of illegal drugs is not their problem. If they would but listen as I teach them how to deal with life and its inherent circumstances, they would never use another drink or snort of cocaine.

Dr. Narramore puts it this way, "Pulling up a weed without removing its taproot gives no guarantee that you have eliminated it. Just so, erasing the symptoms of a problem without dealing with its source may not prevent its reappearance in another guise." How true! Thus, the wise counselor must look for other factors (symptoms) as the counselee is being interviewed. He must also look for precipitating and predisposing factors. As these things begin to surface, the counselor will be able to better help the counselee.

The counselor must never try to "yank" information out of the counselee. He must be patient and allow the counselee to talk. By doing so, he is permitting the counselee to think and reflect upon why he is where he is both physically and spiritually. As the counselee talks and thinks, he will gain new insights into himself, which will eventually lead to new attitudes. I think that in every counseling case, the counselor would be wise to ask himself the following four questions:

1] What is the *context* of this problem?

2] Who are the *persons* involved? (Generally, more than the counselee)

3] Which *environmental factors* are contributing to the difficulty?

4] What *other conditions* are impinging upon the situation?

While the counselee is talking, there will be periods when he will pause because he is thinking about what he will say next. The wise counselor will not interrupt during those pauses. These are important times in the life of the counselee, which may bring clues or solutions to his problem. These are what are called "golden moments." I believe the greatest work the wise counselor can do is to lead the counselee to a place where he can think and talk freely, without fear of being interrupted. This is where he sees the relationship between his past experiences and his present feelings. The insights that the counselee gains here will have lasting value because the counselee himself has uncovered them. He will be more willing to accept them because he was the one who thought of them.

One of my counselees came to me and asked me to tell him what he should do with his life. I smiled and gently told him that I was not the person who could do that. He then replied, "Why not? You are the Psychotherapist! You are the one with the Doctorate!" I said, "Yes, that is true, but I cannot tell you what to do with your life or what job you should get. If I did and it worked out, I would be the greatest person since sliced bread. But if it did not work out ..." He smiled and said, "Yes, I know." That was when I then could let him know that I would collaborate with him to come to a resolution of his problem. I did help him and when I saw him some years later, he was doing quite well, thank you.

Dr. Frank B. Minirth in his book 'Christian Psychiatry,' says, "Regardless of whether one thinks of the entire local church or the one-to-one relationship when Christian counseling is mentioned, and regardless of whether the Christian counselor is a minister, psychologist, psychiatrist, or social worker, certain principles make Christian counseling unique." The doctor then lists the principles as follows:

1] Christian Counseling accepts the Bible as the final standard of authority. Christians do not have to depend upon their own consciences to direct their behavior. They may rely upon the Word of God. Thus, Christian counseling offers not only practical guidelines through the Bible, but it points to the one final standard of authority – the Bible.

2] Christian counseling is unique because it depends not only on man's willpower to be responsible but also on God's enabling, indwelling power of the Holy Spirit to conquer man's problems. If a man simply depended upon his own mental strength to conquer his problems, he would be an utter failure. His strength to overcome must be centered on the cross of Christ and the Christ of the cross.

3] Christian counseling is unique because even though man does have a basic selfish component, he if a Christian, has a much stronger godly component. It is only through this stronger component, which we call the Spirit of Christ that man can conquer his problems.

4] Christian counseling is unique in that it offers an effective way to deal with the past as well as with the present. In dealing with the past the Christian counselor can point the counselee to Christ and show him that when we *"confess our sins, He is faithful and just to forgive us our sins and to cleanse us from all unrighteousness,"* I John 1:9. Thus, the guilt and anxiety of the past can be put under the blood of Jesus Christ. Then, the counselor can work with the counselee to help him/her live in the present without the guilt of what happened before conversion dragging him/her down to despondency and despair.

5] Christian counseling is unique in that it is based on God's love. The Christian counselor, understanding that the love of God caused Him to send His only begotten Son to die in our place

(John 3:16), will not judge or condemn the counselee but will show him the same love that the Lord shows to the counselor. He will point the non-Christian counselee to the Lamb of God and pray that he accepts the Lord as his Saviour. However, for the Christian counselee, the counselor will help him to come to a proper understanding of his problem and then begin to grow in his Christian faith.

6] Christian counseling is unique in that it is universal. In other words, Christian counseling is for all people regardless of genetic, social, educational, or cultural background. The Christian counselor may not be able to help everyone who comes to him but he can point him or her to Christ who forms the foundation of his or her counseling. Jesus claimed that He would help all who turned to Him with their whole being. In Matthew 11:28 Jesus says, *"Come unto me, all you that labor and are heavy laden, and I will give you rest."* The first step for the counselee to find inner peace is through knowing Jesus Christ.

The last reason given showing the uniqueness of Christian counseling is that it deals with the whole person. If a counselee is depressed, it affects his whole being. If one has been unfaithful to his or her spouse guilt, and shame affect the whole being. The Christian counselor understands the intricate workings of the whole person and therefore deals with the spiritual, psychological, and physical aspects of each individual's problem. If the counselor denies the reality of any of the dimensions of man, he has limited himself to dealing with only one or two aspects of a problem and this is tragic for the counselee because he is not getting all of the available help. Man is a whole, composed of more than one part, and he must be treated as such. *"And the very God of peace sanctify you wholly; I pray God your whole spirit and soul and body be preserved blameless unto the coming of our Lord Jesus Christ,"* I Thessalonians 5:23.

Conversation for Change

In the book, 'How to Counsel from Scripture,' the writers stress the importance of conversation for change. They begin by stating, "The conversation of

Biblical counseling must proceed from the Word and Spirit of God. To counsel the way of the Lord to each particular counselee, the Biblical counselor must:

1) pursue the Word,

2) pray for the leading of the Holy Spirit, and

3) present the Lord's way as revealed by the Word and the Spirit.

As the counselor reads and studies the Word under the guidance of the Holy Spirit, he will be accumulating a treasury of life and truth from which to draw during counseling."

I believe the counselor should have a vast number of books to research for counseling purposes but he should never permit the books in his library to replace THE BOOK (Bible). Should that happen, the counselor would simply become a parrot of the writers and counselors that he reads rather than a God-called counselor who relies upon the Word and the Spirit for his strength in the counseling procedure. The genuine Christian counselor must rely upon the Word and the Holy Spirit rather than the systems of men. Jesus said in John 6:63, *"It is the Spirit that gives life; the flesh profits nothing: the words that I speak unto you, they are Spirit, and they are life."* Again in John 14:26, Jesus tells us, *"But the Comforter, who is the Holy Spirit, Whom the Father will send in my name, He shall teach you all things, and bring all things to your remembrance, whatsoever I have said unto you."* Thus, reliance upon the Holy Spirit is essential in Biblical counseling.

The Bible does not teach a methodology of merely reflecting a person's feelings, but it teaches a combination of mercy and truth. The counselor must be vigilant to keep a balance between mercy on the one hand and truth on the other as he attempts to help the counselee. The conversation that the counselor has with the counselee must be based solidly upon the Word of God.

This section relates to what Jay E. Adams talked about when he stated, "Language is a characteristic of God." God spoke and it was done. Language is the one thing that separates man from animals.

The Biblical counselor cannot just pat a counselee on the back and give him pleasant words that he wants to hear. This will not help the counselee; rather, it will enable him to continue with the present state or worse. The Apostle Paul did not fear hurting someone's feelings when he saw that a direct word of exhortation was necessary. This does not mean the counselor is to be insensitive to the needs of the counselee. However, the counselee needs the words of truth combined with mercy to be set free from the bondages and hurts of the past. The spiritual counselor needs to be able to discern in which areas of the counselee's life the Lord is working and then he will understand what proportion of mercy and truth should characterize his exercise of ministry. The biblical counselor does not overlook sin in the life of the counselee but looks beyond the sin to the hurt and the expression of the flesh trying to meet its own needs.

I quote from Martin & Deidre Bobgan's book, (How to Counsel from Scripture) – "The focus of all counseling must be a profound relationship of love. Every problem can be met through a greater realization of God's love and through responding to His love. As two believers come together to seek God's solutions to problems, they will be examining thoughts, emotions, and actions in the context of God's love and God's Word."

The Bible teaches that *"God is love"* in 1st John 4:8. I contend that the focus of all counseling must be to point the counselee to Jesus Christ, Who is God manifested in the flesh. Simply pointing a person to love may, but not necessarily, give a false impression, but when pointing the counselee to Christ, one can never give the wrong impression. Love is not love unless the person to whom it is given receives it. God has already given His love in the person of His Son, Jesus Christ, but unless the person who is suffering receives it, it is not love to him.

As counselors, we must show the love of Christ by pointing the counselee to Jesus, the greatest lover and counselor of all. The love and grace of God must flow through the counselor to the counselee if there is to be a change in his life.

The many sides of counseling problems

After years of counseling, there is one thing that seems to stand out above all others concerning the problems of humanity. That is, every problem seems to have many sides. This writer contends that it takes at least two or more persons to tangle. While it may be true that the person who comes for counseling is depressed, or is an addict, there are usually more factors or persons involved than the one who requires counseling. The problem may manifest in a day or overnight, but it did not occur overnight. Therefore, it probably will not be corrected overnight. We first must get to the root of the problem and deal with that rather than the symptom. Remember that I stated earlier if the root is dealt with, the symptom will disappear. The counselee's problem is probably the result of years of verbal, physical, or emotional abuse and apparent failure by another party or parties. Even situations that at first seemed to indicate one person was completely innocent while the other was to blame often later revealed that both parties were somewhat at fault.

One story that comes to mind is a couple with whom I

visited concerning a particular situation. That morning about 9 AM, I received a call from the couple asking that I would come back because they needed counseling for various problems they were having in their marriage. This was an older couple, one of whom had been divorced and lived alone for about thirty years, and the other whose spouse had passed away about a year earlier. The couple loved each other but was having problems that they did not know how to deal with. I will call them Ron and Liz, (not their real names).

As I listened to Ron, who began to talk first, I soon realized that most of his problems with Liz were due to the hurts of the past (root), which brought about insecurity in his life. He could only see things his way.

Liz, on the other hand, did not see anything wrong with her thinking about the situation and accused Ron of being jealous of her talking with her son too long. This is only one of the many problems that surfaced but it shows how each person sees only one side. As I encouraged each one to talk, I very quickly saw where the problem originated and began to point them in the right direction. I explained to them the difference between a man and a woman - (not the sexual difference because that was not the problem) - that the man is primarily intellectual and does not always comprehend the emotional side of the woman, and vice versa. As Ron talked, he finally went back to his first marriage and opened the door to his present wife on several things that she did not know. As a result, she began to comprehend Ron's way of thinking in more intimate detail. We discovered that Ron's seeming jealousy was not jealousy at all – it was insecurity based upon his past failed marriage, in which his children were also taken from him. In other words, Ron began to see the different sides of the problem and now he can work on dealing with it in a positive way.

Liz began to see things from all sides as well and most of her apparent problems disappeared before the session ended. Her greatest problem was that they did not do anything together anymore. As a result, they were having more disagreements, and it was not pleasant. The key was to get each to see the other side and understand where each was headed.

They have now agreed to go out on a date at least once per week, as well as take a walk together, at least once per week. This will keep the spark (so to speak) in their marriage. Ron will be working on his insecurities and Liz is happy that they are doing things together again for the first time in several months.

In one counseling session, the counselees were willing participants, and much fruit has come from it. However, not all problems can be brought to the forefront and corrected in one counseling session. The counselor may have to have several sessions to uncover many of the basic causes of the problem presented. The counselor must never permit himself to be emotionally moved by the counselee for if he does, he will lose any opportunity to view the problem objectively.

I have found, that in counseling couples, it is best to counsel one first and then the spouse. After this, both parties should be present for all subsequent counseling sessions. If the problem involves parents or children, the counselor needs to interview them as well; first, individually, and then together, otherwise, he has only one piece of the problem. While this counselor feels that it takes two or more to tangle, he also believes that there are three sides to every story – the two or more parties involved and the truth. To put it another way, 'your side, my side, and the truth.'

In the counseling process, the counselor must, at all times, adhere to the clear teachings of the Word of God. He must never think of himself as a referee because people do not need a referee. They need a competent, trained, biblical counselor. They are looking for someone who can help them come to an understanding of the basic causes (root) of the problem and work toward a resolution of the situation. This will keep the counselor from making snap judgments or decisions regarding the counselee's problem.

In the following chapter, we shall look at a few of the different approaches to counseling.

Counseling Approaches

There are a substantial number of approaches to counseling and the counselor must through testing of his own capabilities come to a resolution of which is best for him. Several years ago, I had three counseling students sent to me from a certain university to do their practicum. Their instructor told them that they were not permitted to do any counseling but to shadow me as I worked. Therefore, I encouraged the students to watch, listen intently, and learn, as I talked with each counselee. My purpose was to show them that I work differently with each individual, as I believe that since each counselee is different so also must the counseling approach differ. What works with one counselee may not work with another.

In talking with the counselee, I would never give direct advice but point out the pros and cons of going in a particular direction. For example, one man came to the office and asked me to tell him whether or not he should go back to school and what school he should study to better his life. My question to him was simple, "What do you want to do with your life?" He then began to talk about his past, what he had lost, how he had lost it, and so forth. I try not to dwell on the past because we need to move out of the past and into the present. The man in my office jumped from the past into the future. Then, by using a series of questions, I had to bring him from the future, back to the present. My question here would be, how is it possible for one to jump from the past into the future without dealing with the problems that got him there and then learn how to live in the present as he makes plans for the future? That question was not posed to him but was in my mind as I talked with him and later could inform the student of my purpose.

I find that some folks bring the past into the present and then project that (with all of its problems) into the future so that all they see for their future is more of the same. This makes for a miserable life.

In my counseling practice, I usually employed (past-tense, I am now retired) the principles of the indirect-directive approach so that the counselee will be helped to gain an understanding of his situation, for only then will he be able to gain victory. I have found that most counselees will solve their own problem if the counselor permits them to talk. The man I briefly mentioned above did not want to do anything himself. He wanted to have the counselor do everything for him and when confronted with this, he admitted to it. The counselor-in-training was astounded by how I knew that and how I could get the counselee to admit as much. Needless to say, I failed with that counselee because I could not do everything for him, and he was not willing to take responsibility for what he wanted out of life. Nevertheless, the counselor cannot become discouraged by the counselees that he loses – he must keep on helping all he can and then he will win some of the cases.

One counselee told me that every time I would say unless he had a relationship with Jesus Christ, he would grit his teeth. Every time I would say that You can do anything you want to do and follow with the question, 'How bad do you want it?' he would get angry. He told me that, that statement is now burned in his memory and anytime he even thinks about the things he was involved with he could never go back there because he still hears me saying those words. A little while later, he told me that he now understood what I was talking about when I said that you must have a relationship with Jesus Christ if you are going to stay free of alcohol and drugs. It does not matter how much willpower one has; he cannot overcome this battle in his own strength. It must be done in the strength of Jesus Christ (Philippians 4:13). That counselee has become a wonderful Christian and enjoys full-time employment. In his spare time, he helps others by counseling them. In addition, he teaches guitar lessons to several students.

In using indirect techniques for a directed end, the counselor must be cautious of two things:

1) He must be cautious that he is not too directive (confrontational), for he may then defeat his own purpose; and

2) He must be cautious that he is too non-directive for then he is not fair to the counselee. There must be a balance between the two. Christ was directive at times and non-directive at other times.

Since the Bible is the Christian counselor's authority and the Holy Spirit his guide, his counseling must be directive (nouthetic). His goal is to help the counselee solve his problems with the Word of God. Thus, the counselor should be able to recognize the counselee's problem and approach it accordingly. The approach is directive in that the counselor should know what the counselee needs to do to handle his problems and how to point him in that direction.

The approach is indirect in that the counselor uses indirect techniques, (questions and statements), to help the counselee reach appropriate decisions. The counselor must ask the counselee questions, which force him to think for himself and then draw his own conclusions. The counselor should also let the counselee know if he appears to be drawing the incorrect conclusion and then guide him toward the right conclusion.

Many counselees focus on the past, but the counselor must focus on the present and why his behavior is such today. It is important to listen to the past, for the past may have some bearing on the present but one cannot shift blame for present behavior to the past. Each person is responsible for his present behavior. The past is behind us, and we cannot go back there to change anything.

I believe I said earlier in this dissertation, (and it bears repeating), that the Bible says, *"As a man thinks, so is he,"* Proverbs 23:7. Therefore, if we think positive, we will be positive, if we think negative, we will be negative. Thus, our thinking determines our outlook; our outlook determines our behavior. We do not feel negative because we act negative – we act negative because we feel negative. When we get out of bed in the morning, we have a choice to be positive or to be negative and we behave accordingly.

There may be unresolved issues of the past that need to

be dealt with but our focus must be on the present and specific plans to deal with the problems at hand. Only then will we be able to prepare to dig into the past and deal with those unresolved issues. It has been said that 'a person does not care how much you know until they know how much you care.' Thus, a counselee is not so much concerned about one's qualifications as they are about how much one cares about them. The counselee must know that the counselor genuinely cares for them and genuinely wants to help them with their struggles. One other thought may be appropriate here – Until one has dealt with past issues and learned to function in the present, he will not be able to move and effectively function in the future society.

The key is insight. Once the counselee gains insight into the true nature of his problem, much of his problem will automatically be resolved. In many cases, the problem is not nearly as big as the counselee sees it. His perception of the nature of the problem must change for the problem to be resolved. Many times, the perception of the problem appears more real than the actual problem itself. In the mind of the counselee, the perception becomes the reality. A crude example may be something like – a person may think someone does not like them but cannot think of a reason for feeling this way. Unless that thinking is dealt with, the person may go through life with the perception that the person does not like her/him and that perception becomes more real than reality to the person who suffers from such a terrible mindset.

Many times, in the counseling process, I have told those looking for help that my office is a safe place. There are no consequences for the counselee's behavior in my office as long as it does not become physical. Therefore, the counselee can ventilate, (I do not encourage ventilation, but I do let it happen if that is what it takes), during which time I listen to him/her, after which I could help the counselee gain insight into his problem. Until the counselee can get his feelings out and get insight into his case, he is unable to formulate a specific plan of action. When the plan of action is formulated, the counselee is then able to work his way through the problem to a successful resolution.

Crises Counseling

Thus far, we have looked at counseling practices and principles in a general way, but at this time, I think it would be beneficial to look at one area of counseling specifically. The area that I have chosen is "crisis counseling" because there is a complete set of counseling principles that must be applied to the person in a crisis. Some of these principles will be applied in the general counseling process but not all of them. In addition, as in the general counseling process, so in the crisis counseling process, what worked for one counselee may not work for another. The counselor must be discerning in his approach to each person in a crisis.

Galatians 6:2 teaches the principle of "edifying" (building up) and helping by bearing one another's burdens. The amplified version of Romans 14:19 reads thus, *"So let us then definitely aim for and eagerly pursue what makes for harmony and for mutual upbuilding (edification and development) of one another."*

Webster's dictionary tells us that *"edify"* means to "build up mentally or morally; to teach, improve." The 20th Century Bible Dictionary adds to Webster's by saying, *"edify"* means to "instruct or improve morally or spiritually; to make strong or healthy." Therefore, our counseling must include edification or 'building up' of the counselee.

Thus, "helping" means assisting a person to do something for his betterment. The question that counselors, psychologists, and ministers must keep in mind while working with an individual is, 'Is my work with this counselee going to cause him/her to grow in Christ and be stronger?' 'Is this person's life going to improve and be better because of my counsel?'

Listening alone is not enough for the person in crisis. With listening, there must also be encouraging words. As the counselee is encouraged, he is being stimulated to do what he should be doing and to think more positively. It is moving him forward toward a better life filled with potential and promise. Encouraging a person helps him to believe he can be something; it says to him that he should believe in his personal worth.

The counselor must have empathy for the person in crisis. He must not "try to have" empathy because the counselee can see through the façade quite quickly. Empathy is one of the most important qualities for effective counseling, but unfortunately, the word has different meanings for different people.

Webster's Dictionary defines *"empathy"* as "identification with and understanding the feelings of another person."

Collins Dictionary defines it as, "the power of understanding, imaginatively entering into another's feelings."

Thus, *"empathy"* is an understanding *of* the counselee rather than a diagnostic understanding *of* the counselee. Empathy requires the ability to go beyond factual knowledge and become involved in the counselee's world of feelings without actually going through what the counselee does. Empathy does not tell a person you understand their trauma or their situation, even if the counselor has had the same experience. For example: if the counselee just lost a child through violent death or drugs, the counselor may have had the same experience but since the two people (counselor and counselee) are different with different thought processes, different cultural settings, and so forth, the counselor should never try to placate (console) the counselee with such words as "I understand what you are going through." He does not and it is a lie to make the counselee feel good, rather than help him out of his downward spiral.

Girard Egan teaches that *"empathy"* involves "discrimination – that is, the ability to get inside the other person, looking at the world through his perspective, and getting a feeling for what his world is like. Not only is it the ability to discriminate, but it is also being able to communicate this understanding to the counselee in such a manner that he realizes we have picked up his feelings and his behavior. The basis of this empathy must be the agape love of God."

Nouthetic counseling is what I have studied and what I have been practicing during my counseling sessions. The term might properly be called "confrontation," but I preferred the terminology of "challenging." This confrontation is not as some have alleged, "having a confrontation" with the counselee who has the difficulty. Rather, it is both the counselee and counselor confronting the issue (problem) together to bring about a viable solution; it challenges the counselees to be all that they can be. I challenge them to change their view of life and to accept God's view of life for them. He said in Jeremiah 29:11, *"For I know the thoughts that I think toward you, says the LORD, thoughts of peace, and not of evil, to give you an expected end."* God has planned that we have peace and prosperity amid a troubled world.

Girard Egan suggests that "confrontation at its best is an extension of advanced, accurate empathy." Norman Wright, about the above statement, says, "It is a response to a counselee based on a deep understanding of his feelings, experiences, and behavior. Such a response involves some unmasking of distortion and the client's understanding of himself, which also includes a challenge to action."

To me, confrontation of the issue(s) that the counselee faces is an act of grace, which involves challenging the undeveloped, the under-developed, the unused, and misused skills and resources of the counselee to examine and understand those resources, putting them to use in action programs. Nouthetic counseling is an invitation by the counselor to the counselee to explore his defenses; those that keep him from understanding and that keep him from action. My purpose in confronting the issue with the counselee is to help him make wiser choices, to help him become more accepting of himself, and become more productive in society. This means that he will be less destructive to both himself and the society in which he lives. Confrontation, (Nouthetic Counseling), is not fun and the counselee can sometimes misunderstand it (yes, even pastors – as one told me - sometimes misunderstand the term). Therefore, the counselor must be extremely cautious about how he confronts the issues facing the counselee. Nouthetic Counseling is the counselor's opportunity to explore growth-defeating discrepancies in the counselee's perceptions, feelings, attitudes, and behavior to compare and examine them. This will help the counselee view his life and behavior in a different light.

Another important principle to follow in all counseling is honesty and acceptance. There have been so many times that I have had counselees say, "You do not judge me. Other people judge me and other counselors just look at me as if they do not want to mess with me. Why do you not judge me?" I then began to let the counselee know that if it were not for the grace of God, I could be in their seat and they in mine. I have no right to judge anyone. God put me in this place where I can help with your problems, and I will if you permit me to get to know you a little better.

Any counselor, if he is to counsel effectively, especially in crisis counseling, must be cautious of several things. Some of these are:

1] The counselor must not be too passive. This will frustrate the counselee, and he will not receive the help he is seeking.

2] The counselor must not be too domineering. In other words, he must not exercise dominance over the counselee. The domineering counselor does not enter into the world of the troubled counselee and he all too often jumps to conclusions that are sometimes erroneous.

3] The counselor must be careful not to talk too much about himself and his personal struggles. Otherwise, the counselee will go away frustrated that he is not receiving the help that he is seeking.

4] The counselor must be cautious that he does not distance himself too much from the counselee. Never prohibit the counselee from crying because the wrong message could be sent to the counselee. The counselee may feel that crying is a sign of weakness if prohibited. The counselor must also be careful of giving false reassurance to the counselee. I have seen this too many times from certain ones who want to counsel but are extremely poor at it.

5] The counselor must be careful of emotional detachment. In other words, the counselor should never condescendingly respond to the counselee. The counselor should not respond to the counselee by intellectualizing just because the counselee tries it.

6] Another response that creates distance between the counselor and the counselee is when the counselor uses pressure tactics. Pressuring counselees in crisis to progress at a more rapid rate than they are able will probably bring about a negative response rather than a positive one, which could be detrimental to the health of the counselee.

We have been talking about various principles in the counseling process, but eight steps in the crisis counseling process have not been written. I learned these steps while doing my crisis intervention course at work. It is important that I share them here. They are:

1] Immediate intervention – That is, there is an immediate crisis that needs attending. I remember one man who came to our center looking for help while threatening to commit suicide. He had lost everything, was high on drugs, was looking at jail time, depression had set in, and he did not know what to do.

2] In a crisis, the counselor must take immediate action. If the counselor is unsure how to handle the case, he should call the proper authorities such as a hospital, another counselor, or a minister. When someone is in a crisis they tend to flounder, and we must move him or her toward a meaningful, purposeful, and goal-directed behavior. They need to know that something is being done right now – the paperwork can be done later, not now.

3] Try to restore the person to a state of balance by achieving a limited goal of crisis counseling. This will help to avert a catastrophe. At this time, there should be no attempt at personality changes. The person is in a downward spiral and needs to receive a sense of balance right now. Thus, the counselor must help the counselee achieve some form of limited goal – a small challenge that he can handle to give him a sense of accomplishment does wonders.

4] It is important to give hope and positive expectations. The counselor must be careful that he does not give false hope. He must encourage the counselee to solve his/her problems but be careful about false promises that will make things worse, not better. Counselees must understand that there is work to do to resolve the crises they are facing and they are expected to work toward that end. The counselor must let the counselee know that he/she believes in them and with time and work there will be a resolution.

5] I think that above all of the steps to getting the counselee in a crisis back on track, is this step. The counselor must let the counselee know that he is supported. Intervention in crises involves giving support, and the counselor may be the only person giving support at this time. Sometimes all the person needs is to know that someone is there to talk with.

6] The backbone of crisis counseling is called focused problem-solving. The counselor and counselee try to determine the main problem that led to the crisis, and then the counselor must help the counselee plan and implement ways to resolve it. In doing so, other little problems may appear along the way but the counselee, with the help of the counselor, must keep focused on the main problem.

7] This step is called self-concept. This involves A] assessing and understanding the counselee's self-image; B] discovering how the crises are affecting it and how what you do will also affect it. This is the time when the counselor helps the counselee to protect and enhance his self-image. If a person in crisis feels bad about himself and has a terrible self-image it will be difficult to get him out of the crisis unless he is helped to assess that self-image and change it with the help of the Lord Jesus Christ.

8] The eighth and last step to helping a person in crisis is by instilling self-reliance. The person in crisis is at the end of his rope, so to speak. He feels so low that if he died, they would have to bring him up to bury him. He sees no hope for the future. He is crushed. He expects the counselor to heal him and rescue him from the pit in which he finds himself, instantaneously. However, the counselor must learn how to help such an individual without having the individual rely upon him. The person is falling apart but he must understand that the counselor is there to help him in his time of crisis. The counselor is not there to do for the counselee what the counselee can do for himself – the counselee must be part of the planning – he must put in some effort to get over the crisis in his life.

The counselor must keep in mind that he cannot be with the client twenty-four hours per day. He must do all he can to ensure that the counselee becomes self-reliant rather than counselor reliant. This is especially true in crisis counseling. It may be difficult for the counselee to break from resting too heavily upon the counselor, but it may also be difficult for the counselor to make sure the counselee begins to stand on his own two feet, so to speak.

I remember quite vividly a particular counselee who had in the past tried to commit suicide. However, I was not made aware of the situation until after his death. The young counselor who had done the paperwork simply overlooked what the counselee had written because the counselee looked so bright and cheerful. He always had a smile on his face and seemed that he was available to help anyone who needed help, at any time. Friday afternoon as I left for home, I said my farewell to this young man and several others of my clients who were folding blankets that I had delivered from one of the large hotel chains.

Everything seemed fine. There was no indication that this man was about to end his life. I did not see the signs. Saturday morning I was going to go to work but decided to change my mind and stay at home. After all, I had already worked more than my normal forty hours. However, at about 11 AM, I received a call telling me to come because one of my clients was found in his bed, dead. I went into the office that day with a heavy heart and many questions.

Could I have done something to prevent this from happening? What happened, and why? Where was the duty counselor? How could I help the rest of the clients as well as the many homeless folks who stayed there for the night? I had never dealt with this type of crisis before nor had I talked with anyone who had dealt with something similar.

Before leaving for the office, I called 911 to say what had happened. I then called one of the officers of the Centre with whom I worked. When that was done, I left for work and when I arrived, the scene before me was one of chaos. The police were already present and waiting on the Medical Examiner. I spent time with the police and then went to get everyone together for a special meeting and explanation at noon and again at 3 P.M. after which

I began to talk with my clients, especially the one who had found the man in his bed.

I felt that if I could keep everyone calm, they would get through this, which I did by spending several hours with them. I then had my former boss, a Wesleyan pastor, spend several more hours counseling those who were most affected by the tragedy. I found that the most important thing to do was to stay calm and focused. As I focused the attention of my counselees on the positive things related to this young man, they overcame their fears and their anger about what had happened. Today, several of them are leading productive lives in society.

I have found that counselees need counselors who can help them look for a solution to their crises. For counseling to be effective, it must be biblical and it must enable the counselee to focus on a resolution to his problem or crises. In the words of Carroll A. Wise, *"Sometimes a counselor can help a person by focusing his attention on some particular aspect of his problem. This should not be done authoritatively but by such a question as, 'Can you talk more about this aspect of your experience?' Such a question leaves the counselee free, provided the relationship is such, to say, 'Yes, I can talk about it,' or 'No, I cannot talk about it.' The counselee is therefore not under pressure to move into something that he is not yet able to discuss."*

One young man called me from the Detox center to ask if I had a place in my program to help him get his life back together. I then told him that since I did not know who he was or what his temperament was like I could not say 'yes' to taking him into the program. However, if he was willing to come to the Centre, I would promise him that he would not be out on the street but that he would have a roof over his head and three meals a day.

He then told me this story. Because of his excessive use of drugs and alcohol, he lost his marriage, his job, and his home. He was now sleeping under a bridge in the bushes and he was in a crisis. He intended to climb the bridge, then jump off and commit suicide but as he began to move in that direction, he said he felt someone inside him say, 'Go call the detox center.' Normally, it would take from a week to two weeks to get someone into detox but the person who answered the phone said, 'Come on over, we have a bed for you.'

The man spent five days in detox and was now being discharged with nowhere to go but back in the bushes. He said that he had called every other program center in the province but they were all full. The last place he called was the Centre because he was not interested in any of that religious stuff. He came as I had asked him and stayed in the homeless shelter for two weeks.

I finally accepted him into the program for addictions and he became one of my best counselees. He now is a born-again believer in Christ and works in the food room of the same center on a full-time basis. He is a success story. One who had been in a crisis is now helping others for the glory of God!

Counseling and Inner Attitudes
– Change

A definite religious resource for the Christian counselor in his counseling work is Jesus' insistence on the necessity of correcting inner attitudes. Jesus could not accept the emphasis on external behavior. He was vitally concerned with what was going on in the depth of a man's soul. This was part of His emphasis on the sacredness of personality. In His insistence on changing inner attitudes, Jesus would find modern Christian psychotherapists in close agreement with Him.

Good counseling, as we have already discovered, does not involve a lecture to people about the necessity of changing their attitudes. This need for change is implicit in the entire counseling process. The counselee comes for help because he recognizes the need for a change. He may not fully appreciate the meaning of such a change but he realizes that it is needed. I think that if the counselor were to try to explain this to the counselee it would create profound anxiety. However, the wise Christian counselor, understanding the situation, knowing that behavior does change when inner attitudes are changed and that people have a capacity for changing their attitudes when negative feelings are worked through in a positive relationship – the counselor knowing these things quietly sets up a relationship, which makes the change of inner attitudes gradually possible. The Christian counselor does not assume the counselee can make these changes by sheer force of his will. He understands those changes take place only after proper conditions have been met, (the counselee's beliefs and thinking have changed sufficiently), and he seeks to set up conditions, which encourage and make change possible.

Again, I refer back to Proverbs 23:7, *"As he thinks in his heart, so is he..."* In other words, man is what he thinks he is. Thus, he must change his attitude before he can change his conduct. When the counselee comes for help, it is because he understands that his attitude or behavior is not right and he wants to change it but does not know how. He, therefore, asks the counselor to help him find the solution to his behavioral problem. Oftentimes, the counselee will come with an expectation that the Christian counselor will advise him concerning his behavior. The Biblical counselor must, without being authoritarian, impress upon the counselee that as his beliefs and thinking changes, so also will his inner attitudes be changed, and his old forms of behavior will no longer be suitable. *"New wine cannot be put into old wineskins"* (cf. Matthew 9:17; Mark 2:22; Luke 5:37). The Christian counseling process must utilize the principle that a change in inner attitude is essential to the cure of illness. The external behavior, which is bothersome to a person or his associates, is but *a* symptom of inner difficulties. Any kind of real therapy involves working the problem out from within the person in terms of his own dynamics.

Change always disturbs the status quo. It always calls for us to get out of our comfort zone. In one of the churches where I pastored, I preached a message on *"change"* but before starting, I asked the congregation how many liked changes. The fact is, no one likes change, yet we know that if we are going to do any kind of productive work or grow in wisdom and knowledge, there must be change. People are creatures of habit – we like things the way they are! Dr. Jay E. Adams says, "Counselors who think of their own comfort, who will not take risks, really do not care enough for their counselees or for God, to do the arduous work of growing. Growing always means abandoning the old ways in favor of new ones." That is the emphasis of II Corinthians 5:17, *"Therefore if any man is in Christ, he is a new creation: old things are passed away; behold all things are become new."*

Solution-focused Counseling

Christian counseling must focus on finding the solution to the problem and must point the counselee in the direction of the solution. Charles Kollar says that there are three rules, which have been formulated to help the counselor stay focused on solutions. These are:

1. If it is not broken, do not fix it!

2. Once you know what works, do more of it!

3. If it does not work, do not do it again. Do something different!

I once counseled a pastor whose church had grown to more than double in size. Then the pastor thought he would start changing certain things, (which I will not mention here as it would probably identify the pastor), and if the people did not conform they could not participate in any form of ministry in the church – ludicrous (I can say that because I knew both the pastor and the church congregation and there was no sin involved – some changes are necessary, others are not)! I repeat, the number one statement above – *"If it is not broken – don't fix it."* Since the church had grown and was continuing to grow, something must have been working right. My advice was (in a nutshell) to leave well enough alone as it related to the changes he wanted to make. He had asked two other seasoned pastors about what he wanted to do, and they gave him the same advice I had given him. However, he was not satisfied and decided to change things anyway. As a result, the church grew down until it could no longer adequately support him.

Finally, the pastor resigned. The counselor needs to always keep all three rules in mind while counseling, especially rule number one, not as a rule but as a guideline. Afterward, that pastor called several other times, questioning what to do, I suggested that he not ask me anymore because he had his mind made up and was determined to do his own thing (I could not let him know I had discovered that he talked with two other pastors, asking the same question and received the same advice that I had given him). This first guideline reminds the counselor to find out what the counselee wants. Many times, the counselor may be put into the position of expert but that is not an outstanding position to be put into. Thus, if the counselee puts the counselor into that position, the counselor should never view himself as such. The counselor may be an expert in the field of counseling, but he is not an expert on any particular counselee, nor is he an expert concerning all phases of counseling. Therefore, the counselor must remain focused on why (the goal of) the counselee came to him for help. How can the reason or goal be utilized to create a resolution?

The second guideline says, *"Once you have found what works, do more of it."* This sounds like good advice. Much, if not all, of the counselor's training has been to look for what is wrong and then try to fix it. The difficulty with this is getting two people to agree together on what the problem is.

I am a firm believer that we should not look for what is wrong. Rather, the counselor should look for what is working in the counselee's life, (in my opinion), and then build on that. If the counselee is a Christian, God is already at work in his life. I have found one of the most frustrating aspects of counseling, whether family, marital, or addiction, is when the methodology becomes problem focused. Regardless of our training, we need to specifically train ourselves to look for what is right and what is working for the counselee. When an exception to the problem is revealed, the goal of counseling is more readily clarified. We should endeavor to make our counseling solution-focused rather than problem-focused. This means that we must keep a positive outlook, which helps the counselee remain positive, as he seeks to make right what was troubling his life.

The third guideline that we mentioned is, "If it does not work, do not do it again." One of my schoolteachers continually told us, "If at first you do not succeed, try, and try again." Yes, keep trying but a different way. To keep trying the same thing, the same way, sounds something like the definition of "insanity" – doing the same thing over and over, expecting different results. This, however, is the opposite of our third guideline, which tells us not to keep doing the same thing repeatedly if it is not working – do something different! This means that if the method that we are using to get the message across is not working, change the method. I have often said that since we live in a different society than thirty or forty years ago, we need to change our methods, or we lose the effects of the message – we do not have to change the message – just the method of delivering it. To keep doing the same thing repeatedly when it is not working is like flogging a dead horse, which will stay dead regardless of how much it is flogged. A Wesleyan pastor once told me that he had found the definition of "insanity," which is what I stated earlier in this paragraph. It went something like this: "Insanity" is doing the same thing repeatedly while looking for different results. The wise counselor would do well to take that as good advice so that he will not be caught using the same techniques or methodology repeatedly without getting results.

I think at this point, there is one more thing that should be mentioned, which is that the counseling relationship is positional. By that, I mean, we sometimes describe how the counselee is behaving by using language that depicts the position the counselee is in at present. Someone who is in a willing position has a clear sense of the problem and is ready to work with the counselor toward a solution. On the other hand, a counselee who is in a blaming position usually has a great deal of information about the other person but does not see himself as part of the solution. Others have come to my office for counseling who have been in an attending position. I have found that the person is there because mom, dad (or both), girlfriend, or best friend wants him there, rather than because he wants to be there himself. Thus, he is often uninvolved and uncommitted to the process of therapy. Others see him as having a problem and needing counsel but he has no goal or agenda to express to the counselor. This type of counselee has no plan to get help from anyone. He wants to please everyone else.

SFC (solution-focused counseling) seeks to discover ways so that every counselee can become a willing participant in the counseling process. This is accomplished by coming alongside the counselee's goals, at whatever level of cooperation he may be able to offer initially. The SFC will seek to keep in mind the three guidelines mentioned earlier as a way to stay focused during the interview or session with the counselee. Staying focused is especially important when counseling someone who has been sexually or mentally abused.

In bringing this 'thesis' to a close, I want to use the words of Gary Collins from his book - Christian Counseling. He says, "There is something innately attractive about being a counselor. Many people see counseling as a glamorous activity that involves giving advice, healing broken relationships, and helping people solve problems. Counseling can be gratifying work, but it does not take long for most to discover that this also can be an emotionally draining, demanding work.

"Counseling involves intensive concentration and sometimes brings pain when we see so many people hurting. When these people fail to improve, as often happens, it is easy for us to blame ourselves. We try harder and wonder what went wrong. As more and more needy people come for help, there is a tendency to keep increasing our counseling loads and pushing ourselves closer to the limits of our endurance. Sometimes the counselees' problems remind us of our own insecurities or conflicts and this can threaten the counselor's own stability or feelings of self-worth. Little wonder counseling has been both a fulfilling and hazardous occupation."

In my experience, I have seen so many failures that I have done exactly what Gary Collins wrote. I have, (in the past), blamed myself for the failure and second-guessed my counseling approach and myself many times. In addition, I have overloaded myself with counselees to the point that I would go home from the office completely and emotionally drained. Still, after years of counseling, I ask myself daily, 'Is there something more that I can do to help these people? How can I be more successful in counseling?'

However, now that I have had a few years of experience, I have a greater understanding of the addict's life and how he got there, as well as, what it takes for him to get clean, stay clean, and have a productive life in society. I keep emphasizing that they need a personal relationship with Jesus Christ. It is not enough to know about Him, one must know Him on a personal level. After counseling addicts, counseling believers becomes quite easy. It is just as important, just as serious, but much less strenuous.

The goal is to see lives changed by the resurrected Christ, and so, we must, at all times, find the root of the problem and then focus on finding the solution in a cooperative (counselee and counselor) manner. In all cases, the counselor must never lose sight of the fact that there will be failures and successes in his counseling. Thus, he must focus on the achievements and let the Lord take care of the rest. He/she becomes like a shot (scattergun) whenever one loses focus. It becomes a hit-or-miss proposition! Let the reader remain focused at all times! Amen!

Bibliography

Solution-focused Counseling – Charles A. Kollar, Zondervan Publishing 1997

A Theology of Counseling – Jay E. Adams – Zondervan Publishing 1979

Christian Psychiatry – Frank B. Minirth, MD – Fleming H. Revell Company 1977

Christian Counseling – Gary R. Collins, Ph.D. – Word Publishing 1988

Innovative Approaches to Counseling – Gary Collins – Word Publishing - 1986

Insight & Creativity in Christian Counseling – Jay Adams – Zondervan 1982

Counseling with Youth – Clyde M. Narramore – Zondervan Publishing 1966

Effective Biblical Counseling – Lawrence J. Crabb, Jr. – Zondervan Publishing 1977

Pastoral Counseling – Carroll A. Wise – Harper & Brothers Publishing 1951

Crisis Counseling – H. Norman Wright – Here's Life Publishers 1985

The Psychology of Counseling – Clyde M. Narramore – Zondervan Publishing 1960

How to Counsel from Scripture – Martin & Deidre Bobgan – Moody Press 1985

The Holy Bible – King James Version – B. B. Kirkbride Bible Company – 1988

The Holy Bible – KJ2000 – e-Sword

Webster's Dictionary – Watermill Press – 1991

Collins English Dictionary – Canadian Edition – Harper Collins Publishers – 1989

The P. E. I. Guardian – newspaper – 2007

Psychology, Understanding Behavior – Baron – Byrne and Kantowitz

Personality, Theory Assessment, and Research – L. A. Pervin

The New Concise Bible Dictionary